About the Author

The Zen master SHUNRYU SUZUKI was an unassuming, much-beloved spiritual teacher. Born the son of a Zen master in 1904, Suzuki began Zen training as a youngster and matured over many years of practice in Japan. After continuing to devote himself to his priestly life throughout the Second World War (when priests often turned to other occupations), Suzuki came to San Francisco in 1959. While some priests had come to the West with "new suits and shiny shoes," Suzuki decided to come "in an old robe with a shiny [shaved] head." Attracting students over several years, Suzuki established the Zen Center in San Francisco with a training temple at Tassajara—the first in the West. After a lengthy illness, he died of cancer in December 1971.

About the Editor

EDWARD ESPE BROWN was ordained as a Zen priest in 1971 by Shunryu Suzuki, who gave him the name Jusan Kainei, "Longevity Mountain, Peaceful Sea." While a student at the Tassajara Zen Mountain Center, he wrote two bestselling books, *The Tassajara Bread Book* and *Tassajara Cooking*. His most recent book is *Tomato Blessings and Radish Teachings*.

not always so

not always so

practicing the true spirit of Zen

Shunryu Suzuki

edited by Edward Espe Brown

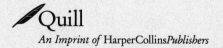
Quill
An Imprint of HarperCollinsPublishers

First Quill edition published 2003.

The Library of Congress has catalogued the hardcover edition as follows:
Suzuki, Shunryu.
Not always so : practicing the true spirit of Zen/Shunryu Suzuki ; edited by Edward Espe Brown.
p. cm.
ISBN 0-06-019785-4
1. Spiritual life — Zen Buddhism. 2. Spiritual life.
I. Brown, Edward Espe. II. Title.
BQ928 . S997 2002
294.'3420427 — dc21
2001051740

ISBN 0-06-095754-9 (pbk.)

04 05 06 07 ❖/RRD 10 9 8 7 6 5 4

Contents

Introduction   *vii*

Shikantaza: Living Fully in Each Moment
  Calmness of Mind   5
  Express Yourself Fully   8
  Freedom from Everything   12
  Jumping off the 100-Foot Pole   16
  Changing Our Karma   21
  Enjoy Your Life   25
  Walk like an Elephant   29

Letters from Emptiness
  Letters from Emptiness   35
  Brown Rice is just Right   40
  The Zen of Going to the Rest Room   42
  Caring for the Soil   47
  Everyday Life is like a Movie   49
  Resuming Big Mind   53
  Ordinary Mind, Buddha Mind   58

Practicing Zen
  Supported from Within   65
  Open Your Intuition   69

Find Out for Yourself   72

Be Kind with Yourself   77

Respect for Things   81

Observing the Precepts   85

Pure Silk, Sharp Iron   89

Not Always So

Not Always So   95

Direct Experience of Reality   99

True Concentration   103

Wherever I Go, I Meet Myself   107

The Boss of Everything   111

Sincere Practice   115

One with Everything   120

Wherever You Are, Enlightenment is There

Wherever You Are, Enlightenment is There   127

Not Sticking to Enlightenment   131

The Teaching Just for You   134

Stand Up by the Ground   139

Just Enough Problems   143

Sun-Faced Buddha, Moon-Faced Buddha   146

Sitting like a Frog   151

Notes about Editing the Lectures   155

Further Reading   159

Acknowledgments   161

Introduction

Always with You

Shunryu Suzuki Roshi died on December 4, 1971. His students at Tassajara Zen Mountain Center had begun a *sesshin,* a week-long meditation intensive, on December first, while in San Francisco where Roshi was staying, a sesshin began at 5:00 A.M. the morning of the fourth. As his students settled into the first period of *zazen* [sitting meditation] in the *zendo* [meditation hall], upstairs in the company of his chosen successor Richard Baker Roshi, his wife Mitsu and son Otohiro, the master left this world. He had waited to depart until most of his students were meditating and would be meditating for several more days. That was a parting gift.

Hundreds of people crowded into the Zen Center for his memorial service, and the next day, I believe, about eighty people journeyed to Colma for a final good-bye. Before the casket disappeared into the fire, we had a ceremony: each person placed a red rose in the casket while all of us chanted. Watching people offer their roses, I was struck by how much everyone loved Suzuki Roshi. Whatever other feelings — calm, sad, frightened, proud, discouraged — may have characterized a person, the gesture of extending an arm and releasing the rose was suffused with love. That was another parting gift.

The first book of his lectures, *Zen Mind, Beginner's Mind,* popularized Suzuki Roshi's expression "beginner's mind" as a metaphor for awakening, a paradigm for living. Keep finding out, don't stick to what you already know: "In the beginner's mind there are many possibilities. In the expert's mind there are few." Thirty years later, *Zen Mind, Beginner's Mind* continues to be one of the world's best-selling books on Buddhism. Now we have edited a few more of his lectures to share his simple yet powerful teachings. "The teaching," he said, "is just for you." Perhaps as you go on your way you will feel Suzuki Roshi's presence in your life: a wise, warm-hearted friend, an unseen companion in the dark. This is what his words have to offer, an opportunity to awaken the teacher in you, your own aware inwardness, "You are Buddha, and you are ordinary mind."

What is most difficult for any teacher, especially a Zen teacher, is to teach without teaching anything. "If I tell you something," Suzuki Roshi said, "you will stick to it, and limit your own capacity to find out for yourself." But, as Katagiri Roshi said, "You have to say something," because if the teacher says nothing, the students wander about sticking to their habitual ways of being. So the temptation is to be brilliant and give out answers, yet that may simply be "gouging a wound in good flesh," as the saying goes. Now, instead of being self-reliant, the students turn to the teacher all the more, and the teacher wonders why the students are so needy and so slow to figure things out. However, in the presence of those teachers who give us nothing to stick to, we sense ourselves awakening. What will we do? It is called "freedom" or "liberation"—we are profoundly on our own—and profoundly connected with everything.

Quite possibly Suzuki Roshi's struggle to speak English invigorated his teaching. Did he, for instance, really mean to say *things as it is*? Was that improper English or was it a teaching? That the expression appears several times in this volume points to the latter. What, then, was his teaching? The more we try to pin it down, the more elusive it gets, yet as disciples and students, as fellow seekers, we often attempt to see if we "got it." Can we express it? Can we speak it? What are the words which will turn our lives in the direction of realization? in the direction of benefiting others?

Would enlightenment help us? Suzuki Roshi dismisses the idea of aiming for some special experience, which will change our lives forever, as "a mistake," as "sight-seeing practice." Yet he does not dispense with enlightenment. This, he says, is "to forget this moment and grow into the next." "Wherever you are," he says, "enlightenment is there." And how are we to experience that?

One thing Roshi keeps mentioning is to "practice *shikantaza.*" Commonly translated as "just sitting," it could also be described as "not suppressing and not indulging thinking." But Suzuki has various ways to express it: "Live in each instant of time," or "Exhale completely." It is one of those expressions that can be endlessly explained and not explained at all, and certainly if you ever stop to wonder if "this" is shikantaza, it probably isn't. On the one hand, shikantaza points to "this" not "that," as in "Exhale completely, disappearing into emptiness. This is shikantaza." It is exhaling rather than inhaling, disappearing rather than appearing. On the other hand, it points to non-differentiation. To "live in each instant of time" is "to express yourself fully, to expose yourself as you are." Perhaps we could see this fullness as another form of disappearing, a wholeness of being which covers everything. One side is clearing away the monkey mind, the other side is realizing yourself, making yourself "real." So how will we recognize shikantaza, and should we aim to attain it? "Stand up on the ground. Stand up on emptiness." "Shikantaza is just to be ourselves."

The Roshi's way was unfathomable. His teaching was not to

stick to anything, and in his teaching he did not stick to any one way. Here are some stories by way of example.

One day Suzuki Roshi told me to sit right in front of him in the meditation hall "so when you fall asleep and start nodding, I will notice right away and I can get up and hit you." He would use his short wooden stick for the hitting, and I would wake up. At least for a few moments the air and my mind would be clear, still, and quiet, yet vibrant and awake. I felt honored that he cared enough to get up from his meditation and hit me. I would have been sitting quite straight and alert for about thirty minutes before nodding off, and then he would be there: *Wap-wap! Wap-wap!* As a Zen student, he said, "you should try to meet someone who is as sincere as you."

Everything would drop away. Before his double striking of the shoulders, his stick would rest briefly on the shoulder just to the right of the neck, and we would place our palms together and bow, leaning forward with our head tilted to the left. Then after he had struck the right shoulder, we would lean to the right to receive his blows on the left. The blows themselves were inconceivably sudden and striking, not in the sense that they were physically intimidating, but they could not be anticipated or timed, so no thought, feeling, or sensation could stand up to them. Rather than knocking some sense into you, it was more like knocking the floor out from under you. This could be quite unsettling, but on the other hand quite grounding. For a few moments one could taste freedom from everything, a sense of spaciousness. "Don't stick to anything," he said, "not even the truth." "When you practice as though this were your last moment, you will have freedom from everything." Then sooner or later there would be a groping around for something to grasp, something to focus on, something to do something about. The world of things would reappear—something to deal with and obsess about. How's it going?

Other times when I struggled to sit still, Suzuki Roshi's hands would rest motionlessly on my shoulders, touching me through and through. My breath would soften and lengthen. Tension would release, and my shoulders would start to radiate with warmth and vitality. Once I asked him what he was doing when he had his hands on my shoulders, and he said, "I'm meditating with you."

It's quite rare to be touched like that, receptively and openly, with kind regard. Most touch says, "Go over there" or "Get over here," "Straighten up" or "Calm down." This touch said, "I'll be here with you wherever you are. I'm willing to touch whatever it is." That was the spirit of his meditation, the spirit of his teaching, "Sit with everything. Be one with everything." Innumerable people were touched by Suzuki Roshi's presence and by his teaching, each of us in our own way responded to his kind and upright regard, his meditating with us.

On yet another occasion, after months of struggling with involuntary movements during meditation, I finally decided to "go with the movements" rather than trying to stop them by "getting a grip on things." For most of a period of meditation I sat swirling around this way and that, sensing a spiral of energy rising from the base of my spine. Then with about ten minutes left in the period I heard Suzuki's voice in my ear, "Do *kinhin*." I was annoyed that he had asked me to do walking meditation while everyone else was sitting, so I whispered back, "What?!" Again he simply said, "Do kinhin." So I got up and practiced walking meditation for the rest of the period, calming down to some degree.

Later I went to speak with him. He had never before asked me to do kinhin during zazen, so I thought that perhaps "going with the movements" was not a good thing to do. I told him that I was no longer trying to stop the movements; that I had decided to see what I could find out about the movements by going with them.

But that morning, the first time I tried this out, he asked me to do kinhin. So was it okay to find out about the movements or should I go back to trying to stop them? "Oh," he responded, "that's a very good idea to see what you can find out about the movements. I didn't realize that's what you were doing. That's quite all right." A flood of relief washed through me, and I thought, "I can do this. I'll figure it out."

So I leave it to you to find your way, to explore the range and scope of Suzuki Roshi's teaching, to encounter his firmness and fierceness, his devotion and tenderness, his wisdom and humor. And now and again we can remind ourselves that anything we say about Suzuki and his teaching we are saying about ourselves. We are extraordinary people living extraordinary lives, with innumerable everyday opportunities to practice enlightenment or to enlighten our practice. And let's not forget "the most important thing." It was a phrase Suzuki Roshi used often, and since we never knew what was to follow it, it caught our attention and made us sit up and take note. "The most important thing" that comes to mind right now "is to be able to enjoy your life without being fooled by things."

May all beings be happy, healthy, and free from suffering.

May all beings live in peace and harmony.

Jusan Kainei
(Edward Espe Brown)
Fairfax, California
May, 2001

not always so

Shikantaza:
Living Fully in Each Moment

"When we do not expect anything we can be ourselves.
That is our way, to live fully in each moment of time."

Calmness of Mind

"Calmness of mind is beyond the end of your exhalation, so if you exhale smoothly, without trying to exhale, you are entering into the complete perfect calmness of your mind."

Shikantaza, our zazen, is just to be ourselves. When we do not expect anything we can be ourselves. That is our way, to live fully in each moment of time. This practice continues forever.

We say, "each moment," but in your actual practice a "moment" is too long because in that "moment" your mind is already involved in following the breath. So we say, "Even in a snap of your fingers there are millions of instants of time." This way we can emphasize the feeling of existing in each instant of time. Then your mind is very quiet.

So for a period of time each day, try to sit in shikantaza, without moving, without expecting anything, as if you were in your last moment. Moment after moment you feel your last instant. In each inhalation and each exhalation there are countless instants of time. Your intention is to live in each instant.

First practice smoothly exhaling, then inhaling. Calmness of mind is beyond the end of your exhalation. If you exhale smoothly, without even trying to exhale, you are entering into the complete perfect calmness of your mind. You do not exist anymore. When you exhale this way, then naturally your inhalation will start from there. All that fresh blood bringing everything from outside will pervade your body. You are completely refreshed. Then you start to exhale, to extend that fresh feeling into emptiness. So, moment after moment, without trying to do anything, you continue shikantaza.

Complete shikantaza may be difficult because of the pain in your legs when you are sitting cross-legged. But even though you have pain in your legs, you can do it. Even though your practice is not good enough, you can do it. Your breathing will gradually vanish. You will gradually vanish, fading into emptiness. Inhaling without effort you naturally come back to yourself with some color or form. Exhaling, you gradually fade into emptiness — empty, white paper. That is shikantaza. The important point is your exhalation. Instead of trying to feel yourself as you inhale, fade into emptiness as you exhale.

When you practice this in your last moment, you will have nothing to be afraid of. You are actually aiming at emptiness. You become one with everything after you completely exhale with this feeling. If you are still alive, naturally you will inhale again. "Oh, I'm still alive! Fortunately or unfortunately!" Then you start to exhale and fade into emptiness. Maybe you don't know what kind of feeling it is. But some of you know it. By some chance you must have felt this kind of feeling.

When you do this practice, you cannot easily become angry. When you are more interested in inhaling than in exhaling, you easily become quite angry. You are always trying to be alive. The other day my friend had a heart attack, and all he could do was exhale. He couldn't inhale. That was a terrible feeling, he said. At that moment if he could have practiced exhaling as we do, aiming for emptiness, then I think he would not have felt so bad. The great joy for us is exhaling rather than inhaling. When my friend kept trying to inhale, he thought he couldn't inhale anymore. If he could have exhaled smoothly and completely, then I think another inhalation would have come more easily.

To take care of the exhalation is very important. To die is more important than trying to be alive. When we always try to be alive, we have trouble. Rather than trying to be alive or active, if we can be calm and die or fade away into emptiness, then naturally we will be all right. Buddha will take care of us. Because we have lost our mother's bosom, we do not feel like her child anymore. Yet fading away into emptiness can feel like being at our mother's bosom, and we will feel as though she will take care of us. Moment after moment, do not lose this practice of shikantaza.

Various kinds of religious practice are included in this point. When people say *"Namu Amida Butsu, Namu Amida Butsu,"* they want to be Amida Buddha's children. That is why they practice repeating Amida Buddha's name. The same is true with our zazen practice. If we know how to practice shikantaza, and if they know how to repeat Amida Buddha's name, it cannot be different.

So we have enjoyment, we are free. We feel free to express ourselves because we are ready to fade into emptiness. When we are trying to be active and special and to accomplish something, we cannot express ourselves. Small self will be expressed, but big self will not appear from the emptiness. From the emptiness only great self appears. That is shikantaza, okay? It is not so difficult if you really try.

Thank you very much.

Express Yourself Fully

"It is a big mistake to think that the best way to express yourself is to do whatever you want, acting however you please. This is not expressing yourself. If you know what to do exactly, and you do it, then you can express yourself fully."

When you live completely in each moment, without expecting anything, you have no idea of time. When you are involved in an idea of time—today, tomorrow, or next year—selfish practice begins. Various desires start to behave mischievously. You may think you should get ordained, or you worry about what your next step will be. Trying to become someone else, you lose your practice and lose your virtue. When you are faithful to your position or your work, your true being is there. This is a very important point.

Without any idea of time, your practice goes on and on. Moment after moment you become you yourself. This practice is not so easy. You may not be able to continue it for even one period of meditation. You will need to make a big effort. Then you can practice extending this feeling moment after moment. Eventually it will extend to your everyday life.

The way to extend your practice is to expose yourself as you are, without trying to be someone else. When you are very honest with yourself and brave enough, you can express yourself fully. Whatever people may think, it is all right. Just be yourself, at least for your teacher. That is actual practice, your actual life. Unless you trust your teacher, this is rather difficult, but if you find out that your teacher's spirit is the same as your spirit, then you will be brave enough to continue practicing in this way.

Sometimes you have to argue with your teacher. That is okay, but you should try to understand him and be ready to give up your argument — when you are wrong, when you find yourself foolishly sticking to one point of view, or when you are making some excuse. That is how to be honest with yourself. Then you can give up: "Okay, I surrender. I'm sorry."

You and your teacher are aiming to have perfect communication. For a teacher the important point is always to be ready to surrender to his disciple. When a teacher realizes he is wrong, he can say, "Oh, you are right, I was wrong." If your teacher has that kind of spirit, you will be encouraged to admit your mistake as well, even when it is not so easy. If you continue this kind of practice, people may say, "You are crazy. Something is wrong with you." But it doesn't matter.

We are not the same. Each one of us is different, and each one of us has our own problems. Fortunately you have the support of others who are practicing with you. This is not an umbrella to provide shade to protect you but a space where you can have real practice, a space where you can express yourself fully. You can open your eyes to appreciate the practice of others, and you will find that you are able to communicate without words.

Our way is not to criticize others but to know and appreciate them. Sometimes you may feel you know someone too well, and you have difficulty appreciating them because of your small mind. If you continue practicing together, and your mind is big enough to expose yourself and to accept others, naturally you will become good friends. To know your friend is to know something beyond yourself, beyond even your friend.

You may say that when you are practicing zazen, no one can know your practice, but for me that is the best time to understand you. When you sit facing the wall and I see you from behind, it is especially easy to understand what kind of practice you have. Sometimes I walk around the meditation hall so that I can see you. This is very interesting. If you are dancing or talking or making a big noise, it is rather difficult to understand you. But when we are sitting together, you each sit in your own way.

It is a big mistake to think that the best way to express yourself is to do whatever you want, acting however you please. This is not expressing yourself. When you have many possible ways of expressing yourself, you are not sure what to do, so you will behave superficially. If you know what to do exactly, and you do it, you can express yourself fully.

That is why we follow forms. You may think that you cannot express yourself within a particular form, but when we are all practicing together, strong people will express themselves in a strong way and kind people will express themselves kindly. When we pass the sutra cards along the row during service, you each do it in your own way. The differences among you are easy to see because the form is the same. And because we repeat the same thing over and over again, we can understand our friends' ways eventually. Even if your eyes are shut, you know, "Oh, that was so-and-so." This is the advantage of having rules and rituals.

Without this kind of practice your relationships with people will be very superficial. If someone wears a beautiful robe [here he rubs his robe and laughs], you will think he must be a good priest. If someone gives you a beautiful thing, you will think she is very kind, that she is a wonderful person. That kind of under-standing is not so good.

Usually our society works in a superficial, frivolous way. The controlling power is money or some big noise. Our eyes and ears are not open or subtle enough to see and hear things. Most peo-ple who visit Zen Center find it a strange place: "They do not talk so much. They do not even laugh. What are they doing?" Those who are accustomed to big noises may not notice, but we can communicate without talking so much. We may not always be smiling, but we feel what others are feeling. Our mind is always open, and we are expressing ourselves fully.

We can extend this practice to city life and be good friends with one another. This is not difficult when you decide to be honest with yourself and express yourself fully, without expecting anything. Just being yourself and being ready to understand others is how to extend your practice into everyday life.

We don't know what will happen. If you fail to express your-self fully on each moment, you may regret it later. Because you expect some future time, you miss your opportunity, and you are misunderstood by your friend. Do not wait to express yourself fully.

Thank you very much.

Freedom from Everything

"When you are able to sit, experiencing what is shikantaza, then the meaning of your everyday life will be completely different. You will have freedom from everything."

My practice of shikantaza or zazen changed about two years ago, after I almost drowned. I wanted to cross the creek at Tassajara. I cannot actually swim, but the students were enjoying the water so much, I thought I would join them. There were many beautiful girls over there so I tried to go over there, forgetting that I couldn't swim, and I almost drowned. But I knew I would not die.

I knew I would not drown because there were many students, and someone would help me, so I was not so serious. But the feeling was pretty bad. I was swallowing water, so I stretched out my arms hoping that someone would catch me, but no one helped me. I decided to go to the bottom, to walk, but that was not possible either. I could not reach the bottom and I could not get above the surface. What I saw was the legs of beautiful girls. But I could not take hold of their legs, and I was rather scared.

At that time I realized that we never have good practice until we become quite serious. Because I knew that I was not dying, I was not so serious, and because I was not so serious, I had a very difficult time. If I knew I was dying, I would not have struggled anymore. I would have stayed still. Because I thought I had another moment, I did not become serious. Since then my practice has improved. Now I have confidence in my practice, so I have been telling you how I sit in shikantaza.

It was a very interesting experience. I was among beautiful girls, but the beautiful girls could not save me. And, as you know, I am dying because of my sickness, not because of water. When I am dying, various demons as well as beautiful women will be happy to be with me, and I will be very happy to be with them. Everything is with us, and without being disturbed, we are happy to be with everything. Usually it is difficult to feel that way because we are involved in gaining ideas, expecting some improvement in the future.

When you are not thinking that you have another moment, then naturally you can accept things as they are, you can see things as they are. You will have perfect wisdom at that time. When you are able to sit, experiencing shikantaza, then the meaning of your everyday life will be completely different. You will have freedom from everything. That is the main point. Usually you have no freedom from the things you have or see, but when you experience shikantaza, you will have freedom from things. You will truly enjoy your life, because you are not attached to anything.

You become really happy, and that happiness will continue, which is what we mean by non-attachment. Most of the happiness you have is the kind you later regret losing: "Oh, at that time I was happy, but now I am not so happy." But real happiness will always be with you and will encourage you in both your adversity and your happiness. When you are successful, you will enjoy the success, and when you fail, it will also be okay. You can enjoy the feeling of failure: "Oh, this is pretty good—not as bad as I thought!" You will always have enough. You won't want too much, as you did before.

If you come to a great difficulty, like a big mountain in Nepal that looks like it has no passageway, you will know there is a way to get through. Even a hundred-day sesshin is not difficult. Even though you die, nothing happens. It is okay. So you are always happy, and you will not be discouraged. And the kind of life you choose will be different. Before you have right practice, you may want something big and beautiful: the number-one Zen-practice monastery in the United States, in the world—even better than in Japan. But afterwards, the things you choose and the way of life you follow will be different.

Sometimes I give pretty serious lectures. I put emphasis on difficult, hard practice: "Don't expect the next moment." "Don't move!" I am sorry, but I have to say this because your practice looks so weak, and I want to make you stronger. Actually, it is okay that your practice is not so good, but if you are not strict enough with yourself, and if you lack confidence, then zazen cannot be zazen. It doesn't work. What makes your practice go deeper and deeper is the day-by-day effort of sitting.

In China and Japan there are many stories of teachers who attained enlightenment suddenly like this: *"Umph!"* [laughs and snaps his fingers] You may think it was sudden, but actually it was the result of many years of practice and of failing many times. Dogen Zenji's famous words concerning this are, "Hitting the mark is the result of ninety-nine failures." The last arrow hit the mark, but only after ninety-nine failures. So failure is actually okay.

Each time you shoot, shoot with confidence. Then you are sure to hit the mark. "Ninety-nine failures are okay. I will continue to try to hit the mark." Each time you sit, do your best.

You may think that zazen is crossing your legs for forty minutes, but the most important point is to put all your effort, physical and spiritual, into it.

Concentrate on your breath. When your breathing is not appropriate, it is hard to do any physical work. Even when you sew, your breathing should follow your activity. When you lift something heavy, your breathing should be completely harmonized, or else you cannot lift it. It is not so easy to have good breathing. You will need good posture and a good mudra [ritual hand posture] because your mudra is a symbol of your mental state. If your spine is not straight, your breathing will not be deep enough. Of course, it takes time to develop all of your mental and physical effort.

Enlightenment does not come until your mind and body are in perfect accord. If you cannot accept your experience, you won't feel you have enlightenment. In other words, when your mind and body are completely one, then enlightenment is there. Whatever you hear, whatever you think, that is enlightenment. So it is not the sound of a stone hitting bamboo or the color of plum blossoms that makes people enlightened. It is their practice. In your everyday life you always have opportunities for enlightenment. If you go to the rest room, there is a chance to attain enlightenment. When you cook, there is a chance to attain enlightenment. When you clean the floor, there is a chance to attain enlightenment.

So whatever you do, just do it, without expecting anyone's help. Don't spoil your effort by seeking for shelter. Protect yourself and grow upright to the sky; that is all. That's all, but it is a little bit unusual, isn't it? Maybe we are crazy. Some people may think that we are crazy, and we may think they are crazy. It's okay. We will find out pretty soon who is crazy.

Thank you very much.

Jumping off the 100-Foot Pole

"So the secret is just to say "Yes!" and jump off from here. Then there is no problem. It means to be yourself, always yourself, without sticking to an old self."

Why do we practice Zen when we already have Buddha nature? This was the great question that Dogen Zenji worked on before he went to China and met Tendo Nyojo Zenji. This is not an easy problem, but first of all what does it mean when we say everyone has Buddha nature?

The usual understanding is that Buddha nature is something innate within ourselves, and because of this nature, we do something. If there is a plant, there must be a seed that was there before the plant appeared. Because of their natures, some flowers are red and some flowers are yellow. Most of us understand in that way, but that is not Dogen's understanding. That kind of nature is an idea you have in your mind.

Why would we practice when we already have Buddha nature? We may think that Buddha nature will appear only after we practice and eliminate various selfish desires.

According to Dogen Zenji though, that kind of understanding is based on your unclear observation of things. His understanding is that only when something appears is its Buddha nature there. Nature and things themselves are two names of one reality. Sometimes we say Buddha nature. Sometimes we say enlightenment or bodhi, Buddha or attainment. We call Buddha nature not only by these names, but sometimes we call it "evil desires." We may say evil desires, but for Buddha, that is Buddha nature.

In the same way some people may think that laypeople and priests are fundamentally different, but actually there is no particular person who is a priest. Each one of you could be a priest, and I could be a layperson. Because I wear a robe I am a priest, and I behave like a priest. That's all. There is no innate nature that distinguishes priest from layperson.

Whatever you call it, that is another name of one reality. Even though you call it a mountain or a river, that is just another name of the one reality. When we realize this, we are not fooled by words like 'nature,' 'result,' or 'Buddhahood.' We see things themselves with a clear mind. We understand Buddha nature in this way.

"Evil desires" is another name for Buddha nature. When we practice zazen, where would evil desires come from? In zazen there is no place for evil desires. Still we may believe that evil desires should be eliminated. Why is that? You want to eliminate your evil desires in order to reveal your Buddha nature, but where will you throw them away? When we think that evil desires are something we can throw away, that is heretical. Evil desires is just a name we use, but there is no such thing that we can separate out and throw away.

You may feel as if I am fooling you, but it is not so. It is no laughing matter. When we come to this point, it is necessary to understand our practice of shikantaza.

There is a famous koan [in the *Book of Serenity*] about a man who climbs to the top of a 100-foot pole. If he stays at the top, he is not the enlightened one. When he jumps off the top of the pole, he may be the enlightened one. How we understand this koan is how we understand our practice. The reason we believe that evil desires should be thrown out is because we stay at the top of the pole. Then we have a problem. Actually there is no top of the pole. The pole continues forever, so you cannot stop there. But when you have some experience of enlightenment, you may think that you can rest there, observing various sights from the top of the pole.

Things are continuously growing or changing into something else. Nothing exists in its own form or color. When you think that "Here is the top," then you will have the problem of whether or not to jump off. But you cannot jump off from here. That is already a misunderstanding. It is not possible. And even though you try to stop at the top of the pole, you cannot stay there because it is growing continuously.

That is the problem, so forget all about stopping at the top of the pole. To forget about the top of the pole is to be where you are right now. Not to be this way or that way, not to be in the past or the future, but to be right here. Do you understand? This is shikantaza.

Forget this moment and grow into the next. That is the only way. For instance, when breakfast is ready, my wife hits some wooden clappers. If I don't answer, she may continue to hit them until I feel rather angry. This problem is quite simple — it is because I don't answer. If I say *"Hai!"* ["Yes!"], there is no problem. Because I don't say "Yes!" she continues to call me because she doesn't know whether or not I heard her.

Sometimes she may think, "He knows, but he doesn't answer." When I don't answer, I am on the top of the pole. I don't jump off. I believe I have something important to do at the top of the pole: "You shouldn't call me. You should wait." Or I may think, "This is very important! I am here, on the top of the pole! Don't you know that?" Then she will keep hitting the clappers. That is how we create problems.

So the secret is just to say "Yes!" and jump off from here. Then there is no problem. It means to be yourself in the present moment, always yourself, without sticking to an old self. You forget all about yourself and are refreshed. You are a new self, and before that self becomes an old self, you say "Yes!" and you walk to the kitchen for breakfast. So the point on each moment is to forget the point and extend your practice.

As Dogen Zenji says, "To study Buddhism is to study yourself. To study yourself is to forget yourself on each moment." Then everything will come and help you. Everything will assure your enlightenment. When I say "Yes!" my wife will assure my enlightenment. "Oh, you are a good boy!" But if I stick to this, "I am a good boy," I will create another problem.

So on each moment just concentrate and really be yourself. At this moment, where is Buddha nature? Buddha nature is when you say "Yes!" That "Yes!" is Buddha nature itself. The Buddha nature which you think you already have within yourself is not Buddha nature. When you become you yourself, or when you forget all about yourself and say "Yes!" that is Buddha nature.

This Buddha nature is not something that will appear in the future, but something that is already here. If you have only an idea about Buddha nature, it doesn't mean anything. It is a painted rice cake, not an actual one. If you want to see an actual rice cake, you should see it when it is here. So the purpose of our practice is just to be yourself. When you become just yourself, you have real enlightenment. If you try to hold onto what you attained previously, that is not actual enlightenment.

Sometimes you will laugh at yourself when you fall into wrong practice. "Oh, what am I doing?" When you understand how practice goes back and forth, you will enjoy your practice. Real compassion or love, real encouragement or true courage will arise from here, and you will be a very kind person.

We say, "One practice covers everything," which means that practice includes many virtues like the waves of the sea. When you practice in this way, you become like a stone, a tree, or an ocean. You cover everything. Continuous practice is necessary, so do not rest. How to continue is to have generous mind, big mind, and soft mind—to be flexible, not sticking to anything. Practicing in this way there is no need to be afraid of anything, or to ignore anything. That is strictness of the Way. When we are not afraid of anything, we are imperturbable.

To be completely concentrated on what you do, that is simplicity. And the beauty of practice is that it can be extended endlessly. You cannot say that our way is quite easy or that it is very difficult. It is not difficult at all. Everyone can do it, but to continue it is rather difficult. Don't you think so?

Thank you very much.

Changing Our Karma

"The best way is to know the strict rules of karma and to work on our karma immediately."

You become very serious when you have a big problem, without realizing that you are always creating problems. With a smaller problem, you think, "Oh, this is no trouble, so I can manage it quite easily." You may think this without even knowing how you will cope with the problem you have.

The other day Tatsugami Roshi said, "A tiger catches a mouse with his whole strength." A tiger does not ignore or slight any small animal. The way he catches a mouse and the way he catches and devours a cow are the same. But usually, although you have many problems, you think they are minor, so you don't think it is necessary to exert yourself.

That is the way many countries treat their international problems: "This is a minor problem. As long as we do not violate international treaties, it will be okay. As long as we do not use atomic weapons, we can fight." But that kind of small fight eventually will result in a big fight. So even though the problems you have in your everyday life are small, unless you know how to solve them you will have big difficulties. This is the law of karma. Karma starts from small things, but with neglect your bad karma will accelerate.

Recently I read some of Buddha's teaching about the Way: "Brethren, restrain your many desires while receiving food and drink, accept it as medicine. Do not accept or reject it based on what you like or dislike. Just support your bodies and avoid starvation and thirst. As a bee in gathering honey tastes the flower, but does not harm its color or scent, so brethren, you may accept just enough of people's offerings to avoid distress. Don't have many demands and thereby break their good hearts. Wise men, for example, having judged the capacity of their animals' strength, do not wear them out by overloading them."

"To restrain your many desires" is not really a matter of big or small, many or few. The idea is to go beyond desires. To have few desires means not to divide our concentration among too many things. To do things with oneness of mind, with true-hearted spirit—that is to have few desires.

"While receiving food and drink, accept it as medicine." This means to be concentrated, accepting it with your whole body and mind, without any dualistic idea of "you" and "food." So we "receive" or "accept" food rather than saying that we "take" food. Taking is more dualistic. Accepting is a more complete activity. You may think that "to take" is a more complete action than "to accept." But according to Buddha's teaching, to grasp or take food does not include complete acceptance. Because it is dualistic, you will create karma. You may wish to grasp it because some other person wants to take it, so you must be very quick! But when you receive it, already you have it, and if you accept it with great appreciation —"Thank you very much"—that is what Buddha meant as the true activity of restraining your desires.

"Do not accept or reject it based on what you like or dislike." Again, to accept or reject in this way is dualistic. This kind of teaching does not mean to have control over your desires. If you want to control your desires, you will struggle with how much to

CHANGING OUR KARMA 23

limit your desires or your food, and in that way you will make more problems, one after another. You may even find some good excuse to have more food. Then you will lose your way.

"Just support your bodies and avoid starvation and thirst." If you know how to practice zazen, then you will know how much food to take, and there is no danger of eating too much or too little.

"As a bee in gathering honey tastes the flower but does not harm its color or scent." This is a very famous parable. When we take honey because the flower is beautiful or the scent is nice, we miss the true taste of the flower. When you are taking care of yourself and the flower, you can have a direct feeling of the flower and taste its honey. Often we are not so careful. We may ruin a beautiful flower or we may stick to a particular flower. If we stick too much, eventually the flower will die. The purpose of the flower having honey is to help the plant by inviting bees. So it is necessary to know whether we are like a bee or like something else. When we are aware of the difficulties that we sometimes create, we can extend our practice more carefully throughout our everyday life.

Our minds should be more careful, more attentive, and more reflective. You may think our way has too many rules about how to treat things. But before you know what you are doing, you cannot say there are too many rules. So notice whether you are creating problems in your everyday life or creating bad karma for yourself and for others. And you should also know why you suffer right now. There is a reason why you suffer, and it is not possible to escape from suffering unless you change your karma.

When you follow karma and drive karma in a good direction, you can avoid the destructive nature of karma. You can do that by being attentive to the nature of karma and the nature of your desires and activities. As Buddha pointed out, to know the cause of suffering is to know how to avoid suffering. If you study why you suffer, you will understand cause and effect, and how bad actions result in bad effects. Because you understand, you can avoid the destructive power of karma.

As long as we have an idea of self, karma has an object to work on, so the best way is to make karma work on the voidness of space. If we have no idea of self, karma doesn't know what to do — "Ohhh, where is my partner, where is my friend?" Some people try hard to banish karma, but I don't think that is possible. The best way is to know the strict rules of karma and to work on our karma immediately.

If you know something is wrong with your car, stop your car immediately and work on it. But usually we don't. "Oh, this is a minor problem for my car. It is still running. Let's go." That is not our way. Even though we can keep driving, we should take care of our car very carefully. If you push your car to the limit, the problems are constantly working on your car, until finally it stops. Now it may be too late to fix it, and it will require a lot more energy.

So everyday care is very important. Then you can get rid of your misunderstandings and know what you are actually doing.

Thank you very much.

Enjoy Your Life*

"The only way is to enjoy your life. Even though you are practicing zazen, counting your breath like a snail, you can enjoy your life, maybe much better than making a trip to the moon. That is why we practice zazen. The kind of life you have is not so important. The most important thing is to be able to enjoy your life without being fooled by things."

If you go to a library you will see many books, and you can find out about our human knowledge that is so vast it is almost impossible to study. Now someone is going to land on the moon. Actually I don't know anything about how we are reaching the moon or what kind of feeling we will have when someone arrives there. To me it is not such an interesting thing.

I want to speak about the moon trip, but I have not had any time to study it. So if I talk about the moon trip you may think, "He is so ignorant." People I see today or tomorrow may speak about the moon trip as if they know everything about it. If I hear them speak about the moon trip, and I feel that they are not really interested, I may not respect them so much.

The first one to arrive on the moon may be very proud of his achievement, but I do not think he is a great hero. I don't know

*Note: This lecture was given July 20, 1969, the day Apollo 11 landed on the moon.

how you feel, but I don't feel that way. On television he may be a great hero for a time and be treated that way for his achievement. If we think about this, we immediately know how important it is to practice zazen. Instead of seeking for some success in the objective world, we try to experience the everyday moments of our life more deeply. That is the purpose of zazen.

One time Marian [Derby] showed me some sand. When she gave it to me, she said, "These are very interesting stones." It just looked like sand, but she asked me to look through a magnifying glass. Then those small stones were as interesting as the stones I have in my office. The stones in my office are bigger, but under the glass the sand was quite similar.

If you say, "This is a rock from the moon," you will be very much interested in it. Actually I don't think there is a great difference between rocks we have on the earth and those on the moon. Even if you go to Mars, I think you will find the same rocks. I am quite sure about it. So if you want to find something interesting, instead of hopping around the universe like this, enjoy your life in every moment, observe what you have now, and truly live in your surroundings.

Yesterday I went to visit an island owned by the Nature Conservancy where there are many kinds of animals, birds, and fish. It was a very interesting place. If you live in an area like that and really start to see things, to see the plants and animals in that area, you may want to stay there your whole life. It is such an interesting place. But we human beings go hopping around, ignoring many interesting things. We may even travel to the moon or beyond. It is rather foolish. If you stay in one place, you can enjoy your life completely. That is a more human life.

When we go to the moon I am not sure we are following the best direction for human beings. I don't know what we are doing. When we find the spirit of zazen, we find the way of life to follow as a human being. In other words, we are not fooled by things or fooled by some particular idea. Dogen Zenji at first refused to receive an honorary purple robe from the Emperor. After he turned it down a second time the Emperor said, "You must receive it." So finally he accepted it. But he didn't wear it, and he wrote to the Emperor saying, "I very much appreciate your purple robe, but I do not dare wear it, because if I wore it, the birds and monkeys on this mountain would laugh at me."

In meditation we sometimes practice counting our breath. You may think it is silly to count your breath from one to ten, losing track of the count and starting over. If you use a computer, there will not be any mistake. But the underlying spirit is quite important. While we are counting each number, we find that our life is limitlessly deep. If we count our breath in the ordinary way, as we would count the distance from here to the moon, our practice doesn't mean anything.

To count each breath is to breathe with our whole mind and body. We count each number with the power of the whole universe. So when you really experience counting your breath, you will have deep gratitude, more than if you arrived on the moon. You will not be so interested in something just because it is considered great, or uninterested in something usually considered to be small.

Still you may be very interested in having new experiences the way a baby is. A baby has the same basic attitude of interest towards all things. If you watch her, she will always be enjoying her life. We adults mostly are caught by our preconceived ideas. We are not completely free from the objective world, because we are not one with the objective world.

Things change. For the usual person this is very discouraging. You cannot rely on anything. You cannot have anything. And you will see what you don't want to see. You will meet someone you don't like. If you want to do something, you may find that it is impossible. So you will be discouraged by the way things are going. As a Buddhist you are changing the foundation of your life. "That things change" is the reason why you suffer in this world and become discouraged. When you change your understanding and your way of living, then you can completely enjoy your new life in each moment. The evanescence of things is the reason why you enjoy your life. When you practice in this way, your life becomes stable and meaningful.

So the point is to change your understanding of life and to practice with the right understanding. To arrive on the moon may be a great, historical event, but if we don't change our understanding of life, it won't have much meaning or make much sense. We need to have a deeper understanding of life.

We say there is a Rinzai way and a Soto way, Hinayana practice and Mahayana practice, Buddhism and Christianity. But if you practice any of these as though you are hopping around the universe, it will not help much. If you have right understanding in your practice, then whether you take a train, an airplane, or a ship, you can enjoy your trip. If you go to Japan by boat, it may take ten days, and by airplane, maybe ten hours. But if the point is to enjoy your trip, time is not a concern. Even though you make a trip by airplane, you cannot live a thousand years. You only live one hundred years at most. And you cannot repeat your life. So you cannot compare your life with any other life.

The only way is to enjoy your life. Even though you are practicing zazen, counting your breath like a snail, you can enjoy your life, perhaps even more than taking a trip to the moon. That is why we practice zazen. The most important thing is to be able to enjoy your life without being fooled by things.

Thank you very much.

Walk like an Elephant

"Instead of galloping about, we walk slowly, like a cow or an elephant. If you can walk slowly, without any idea of gain, then you are already a good Zen student."

All the teachings come from practicing zazen, where Buddha's mind is transmitted to us. To sit is to open up our transmitted mind, and all the treasures we experience come from this mind. To realize our true mind or transmitted mind, we practice zazen.

Many people seek for a special place, and become confused. As Dogen Zenji says, "Why give up your own seat and wander about in the dusty realms of foreign countries?" When we are sightseeing, we are involved in an idea of hasty attainment. Our way is to go step by step, appreciating our everyday life. Then we can see what we are doing where we are.

People often think it would be best to study Zen in Japan, but this is rather difficult. "Why don't you stay at Zen Center?" I ask them. If you go to Japan, mostly you will encourage them to build more new buildings. They may be very happy to see you, but it is a waste of time and money, and you will be discouraged because you cannot find a good Zen master. Even if you find a teacher, it will be difficult to understand him and to study with him.

You can do true zazen practice here, watching yourself step by step, one step after another. We practice like a cow rather than a horse. Instead of galloping about, we walk slowly, like a cow or an elephant. If you can walk slowly, without any idea of gain, then you are already a good Zen student.

In China at the end of the Sung Dynasty many Zen masters, responding to their students' desires, encouraged them to attain sudden enlightenment using various psychological means. It may not be a trick—I shall be scolded if I say trick—but I feel that kind of practice is something like a trick. So those Zen masters would be good friends with the psychologists who try to explain the enlightenment experience. But originally Zen was completely different from this kind of practice.

Dogen Zenji makes this point strongly, referring to a story about the first ancestor in China, Bodhidharma, and the second ancestor Taiso Eka. Bodhidharma tells Eka, "If you want to enter our practice, cut yourself off from outward objects and stop your emotional and thinking activity within. When you become like a brick or stone wall, you will enter the Way."

For Eka, this was a very difficult practice, as you must have experienced, but he tried very hard until he finally thought he understood what Bodhidharma meant. Then Eka told Bodhidharma that there was no break, no gap in his practice, never any cessation of practice. And Bodhidharma said, "Then who are you? Who does constant practice?" Eka said, "Because I know myself very well, it is difficult to say who I am." And Bodhidharma said, "That's right. You are my disciple." Do you understand?

We do not practice zazen to attain enlightenment, but rather to express our true nature. Even your thinking is an expression of your true nature when you are practicing zazen. Your thinking is like someone talking in the backyard or across the street. You may wonder what they are talking about, but that someone is not a particular person. That someone is our true nature. The true nature within us is always talking about Buddhism. Whatever we do is an expression of Buddha nature.

When Eka, the second ancestor, came to this point, he told Bodhidharma that he thought he understood: "A stone wall itself is Buddha nature; a brick is also Buddha nature. Everything is an expression of Buddha nature." I used to think that after attaining enlightenment, I would know who is in the backyard talking, but there is no special person hidden within who is explaining a special teaching. All the things we see, all that we hear, is an expression of Buddha nature. When we say Buddha nature, Buddha nature is everything. Buddha nature is our innate true nature, which is universal to every one of us, to all beings.

In this way we realize our true nature is constantly doing something. So Eka says that there is no cessation in practice because it is Buddha's practice, which has no beginning and no end. Then who is practicing that kind of practice? Personally he may be Eka, but his practice is constant and everlasting. It started in the beginningless past and will end in the endless future. So it is difficult to say who is practicing our way.

When we practice zazen, we are practicing with all the ancestors. You should clearly know this point. You cannot waste your time, even though your zazen is not so good. You may not even understand what it is, but someday, sometime, someone will accept your practice. So just practice without wandering, without being involved in sightseeing zazen. Then you have a chance to join our practice. Good or bad doesn't matter. If you sit with this understanding, having conviction in your Buddha nature, then sooner or later you will find yourself in the midst of great Zen masters.

So the important point is to practice without any idea of a hasty gain, without any idea of fame or profit. We do not practice zazen for the sake of others or for the sake of ourselves. Just practice zazen for the sake of zazen. Just sit.

Thank you very much.

Letters from Emptiness

"All descriptions of reality are limited expressions of the world of emptiness. Yet we attach to the descriptions and think they are reality. That is a mistake."

Letters from Emptiness

"Although we have no actual written communications from the world of emptiness, we have some hints or suggestions about what is going on in that world, and that is, you might say, enlightenment. When you see plum blossoms or hear the sound of a small stone hitting bamboo, that is a letter from the world of emptiness."

Shikantaza is to practice or actualize emptiness. Although you can have a tentative understanding of it through your thinking, you should understand emptiness through your experience. You have an idea of emptiness and an idea of being, and you think that being and emptiness are opposites. But in Buddhism both of these are ideas of being. The emptiness we mean is not like the idea you may have. You cannot reach a full understanding of emptiness with your thinking mind or with your feeling. That is why we practice zazen.

We have a term *shosoku,* which is about the feeling you have when you receive a letter from home. Even without an actual picture, you know something about your home, what people are doing there, or which flowers are blooming. That is *shosoku.* Although we have no actual written communications from the world of emptiness, we have some hints or suggestions about what is going on in that world—and that is, you might say, enlightenment. When you see plum blossoms, or hear the sound of a small stone hitting bamboo, that is a letter from the world of emptiness.

Besides the world which we can describe, there is another kind of world. All descriptions of reality are limited expressions of the world of emptiness. Yet we attach to the descriptions and think they are reality. That is a mistake because what is described is not the actual reality, and when you think it is reality, your own idea is involved. That is an idea of self.

Many Buddhists have made this mistake. That is why they were attached to written scriptures or Buddha's words. They thought that his words were the most valuable thing, and that the way to preserve the teaching was to remember what Buddha said. But what Buddha said was just a letter from the world of emptiness, just a suggestion or some help from him. If someone else reads it, it may not make sense. That is the nature of Buddha's words. To understand Buddha's words, we cannot rely on our usual thinking mind. If you want to read a letter from the Buddha's world, it is necessary to understand Buddha's world.

"To empty" water from a cup does not mean to drink it up. "To empty" means to have direct, pure experience without relying on the form or color of being. So our experience is "empty" of our preconceived ideas, our idea of being, our idea of big or small, round or square. Round or square, big or small don't belong to reality but are simply ideas. That is to "empty" water. We have no idea of water even though we see it.

When we analyze our experience, we have ideas of time or space, big or small, heavy or light. A scale of some kind is necessary, and with various scales in our mind, we experience things. Still the thing itself has no scale. That is something we add to reality. Because we always use a scale and depend on it so much, we think the scale really exists. But it doesn't exist. If it did, it would exist with things. Using a scale you can analyze one reality into entities, big and small, but as soon as we conceptualize something it is already a dead experience.

We "empty" ideas of big or small, good or bad from our experience, because the measurement that we use is usually based on the self. When we say good or bad, the scale is yourself. That scale is not always the same. Each person has a scale that is different. So I don't say that the scale is always wrong, but we are liable to use our selfish scale when we analyze, or when we have an idea about something. That selfish part should be empty. How we empty that part is to practice zazen and become more accustomed to accepting *things as it is* without any idea of big or small, good or bad.

For artists or writers to express their direct experience, they may paint or write. But if their experience is very strong and pure, they may give up trying to describe it: "Oh my." That is all. I like making a miniature garden around my house, but if I go to the stream and see the wonderful rocks and water running, I give up: "Oh, no, I shall never try to make a rock garden. It is much better to clean up Tassajara Creek, picking up any paper or fallen branches."

In nature itself there is beauty that is beyond beauty. When you see a part of it, you may think this rock should be moved one way, and that rock should be moved another way, and then it will be a complete garden. Because you limit the actual reality using the scale of your small self, there is either a good garden or a bad garden, and you want to change some stones. But if you see the thing itself as it is with a wider mind, there is no need to do anything.

The thing itself is emptiness, but because you add something to it, you spoil the actual reality. So if we don't spoil things, that is to empty things. When you sit in shikantaza, don't be disturbed by sounds, don't operate your thinking mind. This means not to rely on any sense organ or the thinking mind and just receive the letter from the world of emptiness. That is shikantaza.

To empty is not the same as to deny. Usually when we deny something, we want to replace it with something else. When I deny the blue cup, it means I want the white cup. When you argue and deny someone else's opinion, you are forcing your own opinion on another. That is what we usually do. But our way is not like that. By emptying the added element of our self-centered ideas, we purify our observation of things. When we see and accept things as they are, we have no need to replace one thing with another. That is what we mean by "to empty" things.

If we empty things, letting them be *as it is,* then things will work. Originally things are related and things are one, and as one being it will extend itself. To let it extend itself, we empty things. When we have this kind of attitude, then without any idea of religion we have religion. When this attitude is missing in our religious practice, it will naturally become like opium. To purify our experience and to observe *things as it is* is to understand the world of emptiness and to understand why Buddha left so many teachings.

In our practice of shikantaza we do not seek for anything, because when we seek for something, an idea of self is involved. Then we try to achieve something to further the idea of self. That is what you are doing when you make some effort, but our effort is to get rid of self-centered activity. That is how we purify our experience.

For instance, if you are reading, your wife or husband may say, "Would you like to have a cup of tea?" "Oh, I am busy," you may say, "don't bother me." When you are reading in that way, I think you should be careful. You should be ready to say, "Yes, that would be wonderful, please bring me a cup of tea." Then you stop reading and have a cup of tea. After having a cup of tea, you continue your reading.

Otherwise your attitude is, "I am very busy right now!" That is not so good, because then your mind is not actually in full function. A part of your mind is working hard, but the other part may not be working so hard. You may be losing your balance in your activity. If it is reading, it may be okay, but if you are making calligraphy and your mind is not in a state of emptiness, your work will tell you, "I am not in a state of emptiness." So you should stop.

If you are a Zen student you should be ashamed of making such calligraphy. To make calligraphy is to practice zazen. So when you are working on calligraphy, if someone says, "Please have a cup of tea," and you answer, "No, I am making calligraphy!" then your calligraphy will say, "No, no!" You cannot fool yourself.

I want you to understand what we are doing here at Zen Center. Sometimes it may be all right to practice zazen as a kind of exercise or training, to make your practice stronger or to make your breathing smooth and natural. That is perhaps included in practice, but when we say shikantaza, that is not what we mean. When we receive a letter from the world of emptiness, then the practice of shikantaza is working.

Thank you very much.

Brown Rice is just Right

"How do you like zazen? I think it may be better to ask, how do you like brown rice? Zazen is too big a topic. Brown rice is just right. Actually, there is not much difference."

How do you like zazen? I think it may be better to ask, how do you like brown rice? Zazen is too big a topic. Brown rice is just right. Actually, there is not much difference. When you eat brown rice, you have to chew it, and unless you chew it, it is difficult to swallow. When you chew it very well, your mouth becomes part of the kitchen, and actually the brown rice becomes more and more tasty. When we eat white rice, we don't chew so much, but that little bit of chewing feels so good that naturally the rice goes right down our throats.

When we digest food completely, what will become of it? It will be transformed, changing its chemical nature, and will permeate our whole body. In the process it dies within our body. To eat and digest food is natural to us, as we are always changing. This organic process is called "emptiness." The reason we call it emptiness is that it has no special form. It has some form, but that form is not permanent. While it is changing, it carries on our life energy.

We know that we are empty, and also that this earth is empty. The forms are not permanent. You may wonder, "What is this universe?" But this universe has no limit. Emptiness is not something you can understand through a space trip. Emptiness can be understood when you are perfectly involved in chewing rice. This is actual emptiness.

The most important point is to establish yourself in a true sense, without establishing yourself on delusion. And yet we cannot live or practice without delusion. Delusion is necessary, but delusion is not something on which you can establish yourself. It is like a stepladder. Without it you cannot climb up, but you don't stay on the stepladder. With this confidence, you can continue to study our way. That is why I say, "Don't run away. Stick with me." I do not mean, "Stick to me." I mean stick with yourself, not with delusion. Sometimes I may be a delusion. You may overestimate me: "He is a good teacher!" That is already a kind of delusion. I am your friend. I am just practicing with you as your friend who has many stepladders.

We shouldn't be disappointed with a bad teacher or with a bad student. You know, if a bad student and a bad teacher strive for the truth, something real will be established. That is our zazen. We must continue to practice zazen and continue to chew brown rice. Eventually, we will accomplish something.

Thank you very much.

The Zen of Going
to the Rest Room

*"Fortunately or unfortunately, even though you don't like it,
we need to go to the rest room, the stinky rest room. I am
sorry, but I think we have to go to the rest room, as long as
we live."*

How do you feel right now? [laughs] I don't know how you feel,
but I feel as if I have just come out of the rest room. As I am
pretty old, I go to the rest room often. Even when I was young,
I went to the rest room more often than others, and sometimes I
had an advantage because of that. When I went to Eiheiji
Monastery and sat *tangaryo* [a period of continuous sitting for
several days, required for entering a Zen monastery], I could go to
the rest room without a guilty conscience, because I had to! I was
so happy to go to the rest room. I think that going to the rest
room is a good way to look at our practice.

Zen master Ummon may have been the first to make a
connection between our practice and the rest room. "What is
your practice? What is Buddha?" someone asked him. He
answered, "Toilet paper." Actually, nowadays it is toilet paper, but
he said, "Something to wipe yourself with in the rest room."
That is what he said. And since then many Zen masters are

thinking about it, practicing with the koan: What is toilet paper? What did he mean by that?

In our everyday life, we eat many things, good and bad, fancy and simple, tasty and not so tasty. Later we need to go to the rest room. Similarly after filling our mind, we practice zazen. Otherwise our thinking will eventually become very unhealthy. It is necessary for us to make our mind clear before we study something. It is like drawing something on white paper; if you do not use clean white paper, you cannot draw what you want. So it is necessary to go back to your original state where you have nothing to see and nothing to think about. Then you will understand what you are doing.

The more you practice zazen, the more you will be interested in your everyday life. You will discover what is necessary and what is not; what part to correct and what part to emphasize more. So by practice you will know how to organize your life. This is to observe your situation accurately, to clear your mind and begin from your original starting point. This is like going to the rest room.

Our culture is based on the idea of gaining or accumulating something. Science, for instance, is the accumulation of knowledge. I don't know that a modern scientist is greater than a scientist in the sixteenth century. The difference is that we have accumulated our scientific knowledge. That is a good point and at the same time dangerous. We are in danger of being buried under all of our accumulated knowledge. It is like trying to survive without going to the rest room. We are already swimming in the pond of polluted water and air, and we talk about this pollution. At the same time we can hardly survive the pollution of our knowledge.

Each one of us knows how to go to the rest room without attaching to something we have in our bodies. When we realize that we already have everything, we will not be attached to anything. Actually, we have everything. Even without going to the moon, we have it. When we try to go to the moon, it means that we think the moon is not ours.

Our mind, as Buddha told us, is one with everything. Within our mind, everything exists. If we understand things in this way, then we will understand our activity. To study something is to appreciate something. To appreciate something is to be detached from things. When we become detached from things, everything will be ours. Our practice is to realize this kind of big mind; in other words, to go beyond each being including ourselves, and let our self work as it works. That is zazen practice. When we practice zazen, we actually clean up our various attachments.

We are very much afraid of death. But when we are mature enough, we understand that death is something that should happen to us. If you die when you are young, that is a terrible thing. If I die, it is not such a terrible thing, either for me or for you, because I am mature enough to die. I understand my life pretty well, what it is to live one day and what it is to live one year, and what it is to live sixty or one hundred years. So anyway, when you become mature and experienced, having eaten many things in this life, I think you will be happy to die, just as you are happy to go to the rest room. It happens in that way.

An old person, eighty or ninety, hasn't many problems. Physically, old people may suffer, but that suffering is not as big a thing as you think. When people are young they think about death as something terrible, so when they are dying they continue to think that. But actually, it isn't. There is some limit to our capacity to endure physical suffering. And mentally there is a limit to our capacity, but we think it is limitless. We have limitless suffering because we have limitless desire. That kind of desire, as Buddha says, creates our problems. We are accumulating our problems one after another with limitless desire, so we have bottomless fear.

Actually, when we know how to clear up our mind, we will not have as many problems. Just as we go to the rest room every day, we practice zazen every day. In monastic life, the best practice is to clean the rest room. Wherever you go, whichever monastery you go to, you will always find a special person cleaning the rest room. We do not clean our rest room just because it is dirty. Whether it is clean or not, we clean the rest room, until we can do it without any idea of clean or dirty. When that is so, it is actually our zazen practice. To extend this practice to everyday life may seem difficult, but actually it is quite simple. Our laziness makes it difficult, that's all. That is why we put emphasis on endurance, to continue our practice. There should not be any cessation of practice; practice should go on, one moment after another.

Some students who practice zazen very hard are liable to ignore everyday life. If someone attains enlightenment, they may say, "I have attained enlightenment under a great Zen master, so whatever I do is okay. I have complete freedom from good and bad. Only those who do not have an enlightenment experience stick to the idea of good and bad." Speaking in that way is to ignore everyday life. They do not take care of their life. They do not know how to organize their life or know what kind of rhythm they should have. To know the rhythm of our lives is to understand what we are doing. It is necessary to see our activity with a clear mind, through zazen experience.

I came to America because in Japan I had too many problems. I'm not sure, but perhaps that is why I came to America. When I was in Japan, I didn't practice zazen as I do here. Now I have very different problems than I had in Japan. Even though I am practicing zazen with you, my mind is like a garbage can. Even though I am in America, which is called a free country, my mind is like a garbage can. I am a Japanese and I have many Japanese friends here, so I have the problems most Japanese have, in addition to other problems. Sometimes I wonder what I am doing here. But when I know what I am doing clearly, without any overestimation or underestimation, very honestly and truly, I do not have much burden on my mind. Zazen practice especially has been a great help. If I hadn't been practicing zazen, I wouldn't have survived in the way I did. I started my practice when I was quite young. But even more, I started my practice in its true sense after I came to San Francisco.

You may have a pretty difficult time with me. I know that what I am doing is challenging for you. But this effort to understand things from another angle is not possible without communicating with people who are brought up in a different cultural background. To understand things just from a self-centered personal or national viewpoint is our weakness, and when we do that we cannot develop our culture in its true sense. When our culture comes to this point, the only way to make it healthy is to participate in the cultural activities of various human beings. Then you will understand yourself better, as I understand myself and zazen better since I came to San Francisco.

When you understand yourself better and others better, you can just be yourself. Just to be a good American is to be a good Japanese, and just to be a good Japanese is to be a good American. Because we stick to Japanese way or American way, our mind becomes like a wastepaper basket. If you notice this point, you will understand how important it is to practice zazen. Fortunately or unfortunately, even though you don't like it, we need to go to the rest room, the stinky rest room. I am sorry, but I think we have to go to the rest room, as long as we live.

If I were younger, I would sing a Japanese folk song right now, about the rest room.

Thank you very much.

Caring for the Soil

*"Emptiness is the garden where you cannot see anything. It is
actually the mother of everything, from which everything will come."*

Most of us study Buddhism as though it were something that was
already given to us. We think that what we should do is preserve
the Buddha's teaching, like putting food in the refrigerator. Then
to study Buddhism we take the food out of the refrigerator.
Whenever you want it, it is already there. Instead, Zen students
should be interested in how to produce food from the field, from
the garden. We put the emphasis on the ground.

All of us have Buddha nature, and the teachings that grow from
Buddha nature are similar to one another. The teachings of different schools of Buddhism do not differ so much, but the attitude towards the teaching is different. When you think that the
teaching is already given to you then, naturally, your effort will be
to apply the teaching in this common world. For instance, Ther-
avada students apply the teaching of the twelve Links of Causa-
tion [ignorance, will, mind, name and form, six senses, contact,
acceptance, love, attachment, being, birth, death] to our actual life,
to how we were born and how we die. Mahayana understanding
is that the original purpose of this teaching, when Buddha told it,
was to explain the interdependency of different beings.

Buddha tried to save us by destroying our common sense.

Usually we are not interested in the nothingness of the ground. Our tendency is to be interested in something that is growing in the garden, not in the bare soil itself. But if you want to have a good harvest the most important thing is to make the soil rich and to cultivate it well. The Buddha's teaching is not about the food itself but about how it is grown, and how to take care of it. Buddha was not interested in a special deity or in something that was already there; he was interested in the ground from which various gardens will appear. For him, everything was holy.

Buddha did not think of himself as a special person. He tried to be like the most common person, wearing a robe, begging with a bowl. He thought, "I have many students because the students are very good, not because of me." Buddha was great because his understanding of people was good. Because he understood people he loved them, and he enjoyed helping them. Because he had that kind of spirit, he could be a Buddha.

Thank you very much.

Everyday Life is like a Movie

"When you are practicing, you realize that your mind is like a screen. If the screen is colorful, colorful enough to attract people, then it will not serve its purpose. So to have a screen which is not colorful — to have a pure, plain white screen — is the most important point."

I think most of you are rather curious about what Zen is. Zen is actually our way of life, and to practice zazen is like setting your alarm clock. Unless you set your alarm, the clock will not serve its purpose. Every day we must have a starting point. The sun rises at a certain time and sets at a certain time, always repeating the same thing. And we do too, but it may not feel that way to us. Unless our life is organized, we may not realize how important it is to know where to start our life.

As Zen students our life begins with zazen practice. We come back to zero and start from zero. Although we have various activities, the most important thing is to realize how these activities arise from zero. At the moment you decide to sit, it means that you have already set your alarm. When you have enough confidence to make the decision to start practicing zazen, that is zero.

During zazen you may hear a bird singing. Something is arising in your practice. In the same way in our everyday life many things will arise, and if you know where these things arise from, you will not be disturbed by them. Because you don't know how it happens, you become confused. If you know how things arise, then at the moment something happens you will be ready: "Oh, something is arising." It is like watching the sunrise: "Oh look, the sun is just coming up."

For instance sometimes you will be angry, but anger actually doesn't come all of a sudden. It may come very slowly. When you feel anger come all of a sudden, that is real anger. But when you know how it comes—"anger is arising in my mind"—that is not anger. People may say that you are angry, but actually you are not angry. If you know you are about to start crying, "Oh, I am going to cry," and then in the next two or three minutes, "Oh, I started crying," that is not crying. Our practice is to accept things as you accept various images in your sitting. The most important thing is to have big mind and to accept things.

If you practice zazen to obtain enlightenment, it will be like using an alarm clock without setting the time. It will go off anyway, but it doesn't make much sense. To sit every morning at a certain time makes sense. To know what you are doing at any particular time is the most important thing. This is to make effort according to the situation you are in.

Our everyday life is like a movie playing on the wide screen. Most people are interested in the picture on the screen without realizing there is a screen. When the movie stops and you don't see anything anymore, you think, "I must come again tomorrow evening." [laughs] "I will come back and see another show." When you are just interested in the movie on the screen and it ends, then you expect another show tomorrow, or maybe you are discouraged because there is nothing good on right now. You don't realize the screen is always there.

But when you are practicing, you realize that your mind is like a screen. If the screen is colorful, colorful enough to attract people, then it will not serve its purpose. So to have a screen which is not colorful — to have a pure, plain white screen — is the most important point. But most people are not interested in the pure white screen.

I think it is good to be excited by seeing a movie. To some extent you can enjoy the movie because you know that it is a movie. Even though you have no idea of the screen, still your interest is based on an understanding that this is a movie with a screen and there is a projector or something artificial. So you can enjoy it. That is how we enjoy our life. If you have no idea of the screen or the projector, perhaps you cannot see it as a movie.

Zazen practice is necessary to know the kind of screen you have and to enjoy your life as you enjoy movies in the theater. You are not afraid of the screen. You do not have any particular feeling for the screen, which is just a white screen. So you are not afraid of your life at all. You enjoy something you are afraid of. You enjoy something that makes you angry or makes you cry, and you enjoy the crying and the anger too.

If you have no idea of the screen, then you will even be afraid of enlightenment: "What is it?" "Oh, my!" [laughter] If some-one attains enlightenment, you may ask him about the experience that he had. When you hear about the experience, you may say, "Oh, no! That is not for me." But it is just a movie you know, something for you to enjoy. And if you want to enjoy the movie you should know that it is the combination of film and light and screen, and that the most important thing is the plain white screen.

That white screen is not something that you can actually attain; it is something you always have. The reason you don't feel you have it is because your mind is too busy. Once in a while you should stop all your activities and make your screen white. That is zazen. That is the foundation of our everyday life and our

meditation practice. Without this kind of foundation your practice will not work. All the instructions you receive are about how
to have a clean white screen, even though it is never pure white
because of various attachments and previous stains.

When we just practice zazen with no idea of anything, we are
quite relaxed. Because it is difficult to have complete relaxation
in our usual posture, we take the posture of zazen. To do this we
follow the instructions that have been accumulated from the
experience of many people in the past. They discovered that the
posture of zazen is much better than other postures, better than
standing up or lying down. If you practice zazen following the
instructions, it will work. But if you do not trust your own pure
white screen, your practice will not work.

Thank you very much.

Resuming Big Mind

"When we practice zazen, it is not that big mind is actually controlling small mind, but simply that when small mind becomes calm, big mind starts its true activity."

The purpose of sesshin is to be completely one with our practice. We use two Chinese characters for *sesshin*. *Setsu* [which shortens to *ses* in conjunction with *shin*] means to treat something the way you treat a guest or the way a student treats his teacher. Another meaning of *setsu* is to control or to arrange things in order. *Shin* means mind or heart. So *sesshin* means to have proper functioning of mind. It is our five senses and our will, or small monkey mind, which should be controlled. When we control our monkey mind we resume our true big mind. When monkey mind is always taking over the activity of big mind, we naturally become a monkey. So monkey mind must have its boss, which is big mind.

However, when we practice zazen, it is not that big mind is actually controlling small mind, but simply that when small mind becomes calm, big mind starts its true activity. Most of the time in our everyday life, we are involved in the activity of small mind. That is why we should practice zazen and be completely involved in resuming big mind.

A good example of our practice is a turtle, which has four

legs, a head, and a tail—six parts of the body which are sometimes outside of the shell and sometimes inside. When you want to eat or go somewhere, your legs are out, but if they are always out, you will be caught by something. In case of danger, you draw in your legs, head, and tail. The six parts refer to the five senses and the mind. This is sesshin. For one week, our head, tail, and legs are inside the shell. In the scriptures it says that even demons cannot destroy us if the six parts of our body are inside the shell.

In zazen we do not try to stop thinking or cut off hearing and seeing. If something appears in your mind, leave it. If you hear something, hear it, and just accept it. "Oh"—that is all. No second activity should appear in your zazen. Sound is one activity. The second activity is, "What is that sound—is it a motor car or garbage truck or something?" If you hear a sound, that is all— you hear it. Don't make any judgment. Don't try to figure out what it is. Just open your ears and hear something. Just open your eyes and see something. When you are sitting for a pretty long time, watching the same place on the wall, you may see various images: "It looks like a river," or "it looks like a dragon." Then you may think that you should not be thinking, but you see various things. Dwelling on the images may be a good way to kill time, but it is not sesshin.

To be concentrated on something may be important, but just to have a well-concentrated mind is not zazen. It is one of the elements of practice, but calmness of mind is also necessary, so don't intensify the activity of the five sense organs. Just leave them as they are. That is how to free your true mind. When you can do so in everyday life you will have a soft mind. You won't have many preconceived ideas, and the bad habits in your way of thinking will not be overpowering. You will have generous mind and big mind, and what you say will help others.

For example, in the *Shobogenzo-zuimonki* Dogen Zenji tells a story, which was told to him, about an influential person, Ichijo Motoie. One day Motoie discovered that his sword was missing, and since no one else could have broken into his house, one of his own men must have stolen it. The sword was found and brought back to him, but Motoie said, "This is not my sword, so give it back to the one who owns it." People knew that the man who had the sword was the one who had stolen it, but because Motoie didn't accuse him of it, no one could say anything, so nothing happened. This is the calmness of mind we should have, according to Dogen.

If we have generous, big mind, and if we have a strong spirit of practice, then there is no need to worry. Dogen emphasized a sparse, simple life. Without expecting anything, we just practice our way. Many students asked how it would be possible to support the temple or group without any plan, and he said, "If it becomes difficult to support our temple, we will think about it, but until then, it is not necessary to think about it." So before something happens, it is not our way to think about it too much. In that way we have complete calmness of our mind. Because you have something, you worry about losing it, but if you don't have anything, there is no need to worry.

One night Dogen said, "Even if you think a teaching is complete and right, when someone tells you a better way, you should change your understanding." In this way, we improve our understanding of the teaching forever. Because you think it is right at that time, you follow the theory or rules, but you also have some space in your mind to change your idea. That is soft mind.

It is possible to change your ideas because you know what kind of monkey your thinking is. Sometimes you follow the monkey's suggestion—"Oh yeah, that's right. If we go in that direction, we may get some food. Okay, let's go!" But when you see a better way to go, you may say, "Oh monkey, it may be better to go this way!" If you stick to your greed or anger or some other emotion, if you stick to the thinking mind, your monkey mind, you cannot change. Your mind is not soft.

So in our practice, we rely on something great, and sit in that great space. The pain you have in your legs or some other difficulty is happening in that great space. As long as you do not lose the feeling that you are in the realm of Buddha nature, you can sit even though you have some difficulty. When you want to escape from your difficulty, or when you try to improve your practice, you create another problem for yourself. But if you just exist there, then you have a chance to appreciate your surroundings, and you can accept yourself completely, without changing anything. That is our practice.

To exist in big mind is an act of faith, which is different from the usual faith of believing in a particular idea or being. It is to believe that something is supporting us and supporting all our activities including thinking mind and emotional feelings. All these things are supported by something big that has no form or color. It is impossible to know what it is, but something exists there, something that is neither material nor spiritual. Something like that always exists, and we exist in that space. That is the feeling of pure being.

If you are brave enough to throw yourself into zazen for seven days, a little bit of understanding will help your rigidity and your stubbornness. Almost all the problems you create because of your stubborn mind will vanish. If you have even the smallest understanding of reality, your way of thinking will change completely, and the problems you create will not be problems anymore. But it is also true that as long as we live we will have problems. So we don't practice zazen to attain some big enlightenment that will change our whole being or solve all our problems. That is not the right understanding. That may be what people call "Zen," but true Zen is not like that.

In sesshin, we concentrate on having the experience of true practice. Forgetting all about any idea of gaining anything, we just sit here. If this room is too cold, we will make it warm, and if your legs become painful, you can stretch them. And if it is too difficult, you can rest, but let's continue our practice for these seven days.

Thank you very much.

Ordinary Mind, Buddha Mind

"Buddha in its true sense is not different from ordinary mind. And ordinary mind is not something apart from what is holy. This is a complete understanding of our self. When we practice zazen with this understanding, that is true zazen."

The point of my talk is to give you some support for your practice. There is no need for you to remember what I say. If you stick to it, you stick to the support, not the tree itself. A tree, when it is strong, may still want some support, but the most important thing is the tree itself, not the support.

I am one tree, and each one of you is a tree. You should stand up by yourself. When a tree stands up by itself, we call that tree a Buddha. In other words, when you practice zazen in its true sense, you are really Buddha. Sometimes we call it a tree and sometimes we call it a Buddha. "Buddha," "tree," or "you" are many names of one Buddha.

When you sit, you are independent from various beings, and you are related to various beings. And when you have perfect composure in your practice, you include everything. You are not just you. You are the whole world or the whole cosmos, and you are a Buddha. So when you sit, you are an ordinary human, and you are Buddha. Before you sit, you may stick to the idea that you are ordinary. So when you sit you are not the same being as you are before you sit. Do you understand?

You may say that it is not possible to be ordinary and holy. When you think this way, your understanding is one-sided. In Japanese, we call someone who understands things from just one side a *tamban-kan*, "someone who carries a board on his shoulder." Because you carry a big board on your shoulder, you cannot see the other side. You think you are just an ordinary human, but if you take the board off, you will understand, "Oh, I am Buddha, too. How can I be both Buddha and an ordinary human? It is amazing!" That is enlightenment.

When you experience enlightenment, you will understand things more freely. You won't mind whatever people call you. Ordinary mind? Okay, I am ordinary mind. Buddha? Yes, I am Buddha. How do I come to be both Buddha and ordinary mind? I don't know, but actually I am Buddha and ordinary mind.

Buddha, in its true sense, is not different from ordinary mind. And ordinary mind is not something apart from what is holy. This is a complete understanding of our self. When we practice zazen with this understanding, that is true zazen. We will not be bothered by anything. Whatever you hear, whatever you see, that will be okay. To have this feeling, it is necessary to become accustomed to our practice. If you keep practicing, you will naturally have this understanding and this feeling. It will not be just intellectual. You will have the actual feeling.

Even though someone can explain what Buddhism is, if he does not have the actual feeling, we cannot call him a real Buddhist. Only when your personality is characterized by this kind of feeling can we call you a Buddhist. The way to become characterized by this kind of understanding is to always concentrate on this point. Many koans and sayings bring out this point.

Ordinary mind understands things dualistically, but even though we are doing what we usually do, that is actually Buddha's activity. Buddha's mind, Buddha's activity, and our activity are not different.

Someone may say that "such and such" is Buddha's mind, and "thus and so" is ordinary mind, but there is no need to explain it in that way. When we do something, we cannot say, "I am doing something," because there is no one who is independent from others. When I say something, you will hear it. I cannot do anything by myself, just for myself. If someone does something, everyone will be doing something. Moment after moment, we continue our activity, which is Buddha's activity. But you cannot say that this is just Buddha's activity, because you are actually doing something too. Then you may say "I," but we don't know what "I" that is. You try to say who is doing what, because you want to intellectualize your activity, but before you say anything, the actual activity is present. Who you are is here.

Our activity is both cosmic and personal, so there is no need to explain what we are doing. We may want to explain it, but we should not feel uneasy if we cannot, because it is impossible to understand. Actually, you are here, right here, so before you understand yourself, you are you. After you explain, you are not really you anymore. You just have an image. But usually you will stick to the image which is not you, and you will ignore the reality. As Dogen Zenji said, we human beings attach to something that is not real and forget all about what is real. That is actually what we do. If you realize this point, you will have perfect composure, and you can trust yourself. Whatever happens to you, it doesn't matter. You trust yourself, and this is not the usual trust or belief in what is not real.

When you are able to sit without any image or any sound, with an open mind, that is true practice. When you can do that, you are free from everything. Still it is all right for you to enjoy your life, moment after moment, because you are not enjoying your life as something concrete and eternal. Our life is momentary, and, at the same time, each moment includes its own past and future. In this way our momentary and eternal life will continue. This is how we actually lead our everyday life, how we enjoy our everyday life, and how we have freedom from various difficulties.

I was sick in bed for a long time, and I was thinking about these things. I was just practicing zazen in bed. I should enjoy being in bed. [laughing] Sometimes it was difficult, but then I laughed at myself, "Why is it so difficult? Why don't you enjoy your difficulties?"

That is, I think, our practice.

Thank you very much.

Practicing Zen

"The way to study true Zen is not verbal. Just open yourself and give up everything. Whatever happens, study closely and see what you find out. This is the fundamental attitude."

Supported from Within

". . . We are firmly protected from inside. That is our spirit. We are protected from inside, always, incessantly, so we do not expect any help from outside."

In our service after reciting a sutra, we offer a prayer to dedicate the merit. According to Dogen Zenji we are not seeking for help from outside because we are firmly protected from inside. That is our spirit. We are protected from inside, always, incessantly, so we do not expect any help from outside. Actually it is so, but when we recite the sutra, we say a prayer in the usual way.

In one of our dedications of merit we say, "May the two wheels [the Dharma wheel and the material wheel] of the temple go smoothly and may the calamities which the country and the temple may face, calamities like war, epidemic, famine, fire, water, and wind, be averted." Although we say this, actually the spirit is different. We do not observe our way, or recite our sutra to ask for help. That is not our spirit. When we recite the sutra, we create the feeling of non-duality, perfect calmness, and strong conviction in our practice.

If that kind of feeling is always with us we will be supported. If we become involved in dualistic, selfish practice, to support our building or organization, or to support our personal life, there is not much feeling in our sitting or our chanting. When we have strong confidence in our way and do not expect anything, we can recite the sutra with a deep calm feeling. That is our actual practice.

Dogen Zenji also says that we do not have any idea of dirty or pure, or any idea of calamity or disaster, but even so, we have the practice of cleaning the rest room. Even though your face, or mouth, or body is clean, when you get up you should wash your face and clean your mouth. If you think cleaning the rest room is dirty work, that is the wrong idea. The rest room is not dirty. Even though you don't clean it, it is clean, or more than clean. So we clean it as a practice, not because it is dirty. If you do it because it is dirty, that is not our way.

Our belief is that if the Dharma wheel is turning then the material wheel will be turning too. If we are not supported by anyone, it means our Dharma wheel is not actually going. This is Dogen Zenji's understanding, and I have tested whether it is true or not, especially during the war when I did not have much to eat.

Most priests worked to earn some money to support themselves and their families. My belief was that if I observed the Buddhist way faithfully, people would support me. If no one supported me it would mean that Dogen's words were not true. So I never asked anyone to give me anything. I just observed the Buddhist way without working as a teacher or as a clerk in the town office.

I raised some vegetables and sweet potatoes in my temple garden. That is why I know how to raise vegetables pretty well. I had a spacious garden in front of the temple, so I dug up the ground, took out all the stones, and put in manure. Some villagers came and helped me, and we grew vegetables, and we had a good crop.

One day my neighbor came to help me cook. When she opened the rice box, there was no rice at all. I had a pretty big rice box. She was astounded, so she brought me some rice. It was only a little, as she didn't have much rice, but then my neighbors and members of my temple collected rice. I had quite a few members, so I had quite a lot of rice. When people found out that I had a lot of rice they came to the temple, so I gave my rice to them. The more I gave my rice to them, the more rice I was given.

At that time most people who lived in the city went to the farming families and exchanged whatever possessions they could for food: potatoes, rice, sweet potatoes, or pumpkin. But I had no such difficulty. Most of the time I had plenty of food, but I didn't feel so good eating something different from other people, so I tried to eat the same food as they did. Here at Tassajara the food is wonderful, strong and rich, in comparison to the food we had in wartime. So I have not had any complaint about the food. If we observe our way strictly we will surely be protected by Buddha. We will trust people, and we will trust Buddha.

Since the war, Japanese priests have started to wear Western suits, giving up their Buddhist robes, unless they are performing a funeral or memorial service. I don't feel so good about that, so I always wear my robes. When I was coming to America, almost all the priests who were going abroad wore good suits and shiny shoes. They thought that in order to propagate Buddhism they had to be like the American people. But their heads were not shiny. Their hair was pretty long and well combed, rather than shaved off. But even though they buy the best suits and the best shoes, Japanese are Japanese. They cannot be American people, and American people will find some fault in the way they wear their suits or shoes. That is one reason why I didn't come to America in a suit.

Another reason was that I was disappointed with priests who changed their robes into suits to support themselves, when Dogen said we are firmly protected from within. That is our spirit when we say, "We pray that the Dharma wheel and the material wheel go smoothly forever." This kind of ceremony is a way to repay the benevolence of the Buddha and arhats. Buddha and the arhats are people who supported themselves by depending only on their practice. If we pay full respect to the arhats by practicing with the same spirit they did, we will also be protected.

Dogen says, "If we do not practice our way with everyone, with all sentient beings, with everything in the world, on the cosmic stage, that is not the Buddhist way." The spirit of zazen practice should always be with us, especially when we recite sutras or observe ceremonies. It is not a dualistic or selfish spirit, but is calm and deep, with firm conviction.

When we practice in that way, we are always one with the whole Buddha world, where there is no karmic activity, and our everyday life will be protected by the kind of power which pervades everywhere. What is going on in the world of Buddha is just Buddha activity. There is nothing but Buddha activity in the realm of the Dharma world. In that way, we do not create any karma. We are beyond the karmic world. With this spirit and this understanding we observe our way.

If we are too involved in the idea of time or taking care of the material world, we will lose our way. A priest will not be a priest when he is completely involved in dualistic practice, involved in a busy life in the busy, mundane world. Then there are no more priests. Even though priests are there, they are not practicing the priest's way. So Buddhists should be Buddhists completely. When a Buddhist really becomes a Buddhist he will be supported as a Buddhist.

Thank you very much.

Open Your Intuition

". . . To open your innate nature and to feel something from the bottom of your heart, it is necessary to remain silent. Through this kind of practice you will have a more intuitive understanding of the teaching. Not to talk does not mean to be deaf and dumb, but to listen to your intuition."

The purpose of sesshin is to develop stable practice. In sesshin we do not communicate with words, but being with each other is still a big encouragement. Verbal communication tends to be superficial, but when you don't speak, deeper communication between you will be encouraged, and your mind will become very subtle. Staying silent will open your intuition. Just to stay here without speaking for five days is already very meaningful. That is why we do not talk.

When you are involved in a superficial conversation based on a passing interest, your true feeling will be covered. So to open your innate nature and to feel something from the bottom of your heart, it is necessary to remain silent. Through this kind of practice you will have a more intuitive understanding of the teaching. Not to talk does not mean to be deaf and dumb, but to listen to your intuition.

The same is true with reading. When you become interested in something you are reading, your intuition does not tend to open. That is why we don't read during sesshin. It doesn't mean to confine yourself in the dark, but by not reading you will encourage your intuition to open.

Even if you are doing koan practice, it is not necessary to speak or to read. Especially for beginners it may be difficult to remain silent or not to read the newspapers. You may feel very bored [laughs], but you should continue your practice. In sesshin, everything will be taken care of by the old students, who will help the newer students to practice deeply.

Just sit, and see what happens. Try to keep the right posture, according to the instructions, and follow the rules. Following the rules lets you find yourself. The rules let you know what time it is, when to eat, and how to walk. If there are no rules, and no one is taking care of you, it is rather difficult to practice. So the rules will be a great help. It is much better than not having any rules and sitting in a corner of the room five days without doing anything. The rules are not something to restrict you, but something to support your practice.

There are various ways to practice: following the breath, counting the breath, or koan practice. This time I recommend following the breath. When you find it difficult to follow the breath, then counting the breath will be a help. Then you will know exactly what you are doing. If your practice gets lost, you will notice immediately.

When you practice following the breath, don't make too much effort to make your breathing slow down or deepen, or anything like that. If you just follow your breath, then naturally your breathing will be appropriate for your practice, even though you don't adjust it.

Various instructions will be given to you to help your practice. We do not give instructions in order to force you to do some special practice. It does not mean you should do this, or you shouldn't do that. You may have various instructions, but practice is up to you.

Thank you very much.

Find Out for Yourself

"Whatever happens, whether you think it is good or bad, study closely and see what you can find out. This is the fundamental attitude. Sometimes you will do things without much reason, like a child who draws pictures whether they are good or bad. If that is difficult for you, you are not actually ready to practice zazen."

In your zazen or in your life you will have many difficulties or problems. When you have a problem, see if you can find out for yourself why you have a problem. Usually you will try to solve your difficulty in the best way as soon as possible. Rather than studying for yourself, you ask someone why you have a problem. That kind of approach may work well for your usual life, but if you want to study Zen, it doesn't help.

The moment you are told something by someone and you think you understand, you will stick to it, and you will lose the full function of your nature. When you seek something, your true nature is in full activity, as if you are feeling for your pillow in the dark. If you know where the pillow is, your mind is not in full function. Your mind is acting in a limited sense. When you are seeking for the pillow without knowing where it is, then your mind is open to everything. In this way you will have a more subtle attitude toward everything, and you will see *things as it is.*

If you want to study something, it's better not to know what the answer is. Because you are not satisfied with something you are told, and because you cannot rely on anything set up by someone else, you study Buddhism without knowing how to study it. In this way you find out for yourself what we really mean by "Buddha nature," "practice," or "enlightenment."

Since you seek freedom, you try various ways. Of course you will sometimes find that you have wasted your time. If a Zen master drinks sake, you may think the best way to attain enlightenment is to drink sake. But even though you drink a lot of sake, as he does, you will not attain enlightenment. It may look like you've wasted your time, but that attitude is important. If you continue to try to find out in that way, you will gain more power to understand things. Whatever you do, you will not waste your time.

When you do something with a limited idea, or with some definite purpose, what you will gain is something concrete. This will cover up your inner nature. So it is not a matter of what you study, but a matter of seeing *things as it is,* and accepting *things as it is.*

Some of you may study something only if you like it. If you don't like it, you ignore it. That is a selfish way, and it also limits your power of study. Good or bad, small or big, we study to discover the true reason why something is so big and why something is so small; why something is so good and why something is not so good. If you try to discover only something good, you will miss something, and you will always be limiting your faculties. When you live in a limited world, you cannot accept *things as it is.*

Even if a Zen master had just two or three students, he would never tell them our way in detail. The only way to study with him is to eat with him, talk with him, and do everything with him. You help him without being told how to help him. Mostly he will not seem to be very happy, and he will always be scolding you without any apparent reason. Because you cannot figure out the reason, you will not be so happy and he will not be so happy. If you really want to study with him, you will study how to please him, how to make your life with him a happy one.

You may say that this way of practice is very old-fashioned. It may be so, but I think you had this kind of life in Western civilization too, although not exactly as we did in Japan. The reason why people had a difficult time with their teachers is that there is no particular way for us to study. Each one of us is different from the other. So each one of us must have our own way, and, according to the situation, we should change our way. You cannot stick to anything. The only thing to do is to discover the appropriate way to act under new circumstances.

For instance, in the morning we clean. We don't have enough rags or brooms, so it is almost impossible to participate in our cleaning. Under these circumstances it is still possible to figure out something to do. I don't scold you very much, but if I were a strict Zen master I would be very angry with you, because you give up quite easily: "Oh, no, there is not much cleaning equipment," or, "There is nothing for me to do." You are prone to think this way and easily give up. In such a case, please try hard to figure out how to practice. If you are very sleepy, you may think, "It's better to rest." Yes, sometimes it is better, but at the same time it may be a good chance to practice.

When I was at Eiheiji assisting my teacher, he did not tell us anything, but whenever we made a mistake he scolded us. The usual way to open sliding doors is to open the one on the right, but when I opened it that way, I was scolded: "Don't open it that way! Not that side!" So the next morning I opened the other side and got scolded again. I didn't know what to do. Later I found out that the day I opened the right side his guest was on the right side, so I should have opened the other side. Before opening the door, I should have been careful to find out which side his guest was on.

The day I was appointed to serve him, I gave him a cup of tea. Usually you fill eighty percent of the cup. Since that is the rule, I filled eighty percent, or seventy percent, and he said, "Give me hot tea. Fill the cup with very hot strong tea." So the next morning when there were some guests, I filled all the cups with hot strong tea, almost ninety-nine percent and served them. I was scolded! Actually there is no rule. He himself liked very hot, bitter tea, filled to the brim, but almost all the guests didn't like hot, bitter tea. For him I should serve bitter, hot tea, and for the guests I should offer tea the usual way.

He never told us anything. When I got up twenty minutes earlier than the wake-up bell, I was scolded, "Don't get up so early! You will disturb my sleep." Usually, if I got up earlier, it was good, but for him it was not so good. When you try to understand things better, without any rules or prejudice, this is the meaning of selflessness. You may say that something is a "rule," but rules are already a selfish idea. Actually there are no rules, so when you say, "This is the rule," you are forcing something, the rules, on others.

Rules are only needed when we don't have much time, or when we cannot help others more closely in a kind way. To say, "This is the rule, so you should do it," is easy, but, actually, that is not our way. For the beginner, maybe, instruction is necessary, but for advanced students we don't give much instruction, and they try out various ways. If possible, we give instruction to people one by one. Because that is difficult, we give group instruction or a lecture like this. But don't stick to the lecture. Think about what I really mean.

I feel sorry that I cannot help you very much. But the way to study true Zen is not verbal. Just open yourself and give up everything. Whatever happens, whether you think it is good or bad, study closely and see what you find out. This is the fundamental attitude. Sometimes you will do things without much reason, like a child who draws pictures whether they are good or bad. If that is difficult for you, you are not actually ready to practice zazen.

This is what it means to surrender, even though you have nothing to surrender. Without losing yourself by sticking to a particular rule or understanding, keep finding yourself, moment after moment. This is the only thing for you to do.

Thank you very much.

Be Kind with Yourself

"We put emphasis on warm heart, warm zazen. The warm feeling we have in our practice is, in other words, enlightenment or Buddha's mind."

I want you to have the actual feeling of true practice, because even though I practiced zazen when I was young, I didn't know exactly what it was. Sometimes I was very impressed by our practice at Eiheiji and other monasteries. When I saw great teachers or listened to their lectures, I was deeply moved. But it was difficult to understand those experiences.

Our aim is to have complete experience or full feeling in each moment of practice. What we teach is that enlightenment and practice are one, but my practice was what we call stepladder Zen: "I understand this much now, and next year," I thought, "I will understand a little bit more." That kind of practice doesn't make much sense — I could never be satisfied. If you try stepladder practice, maybe you too will realize that it is a mistake.

If we do not have some warm, big satisfaction in our practice, that is not true practice. Even though you sit, trying to have the right posture and counting your breath, it may still be lifeless zazen, because you are just following instructions. You are not kind enough with yourself. You think that if you follow the instructions given by some teacher, then you will have good zazen, but the purpose of instruction is to encourage you to be kind with yourself. Do not count your breaths just to avoid your thinking mind but to take the best care of your breathing.

If you are very kind with your breathing, one breath after another, you will have a refreshed, warm feeling in your zazen. When you have a warm feeling for your body and your breath, then you can take care of your practice, and you will be fully satisfied. When you are very kind with yourself, naturally you will feel like this.

A mother will take care of her child even though she may have no idea how to make her baby happy. Similarly, when you take care of your posture and your breathing, there is a warm feeling in it. When you have a warm feeling in your practice, that is a good example of the great mercy of Buddha. Whether you are a priest or a layperson, this practice will extend to your everyday life. When you take the utmost care of what you do, then you feel good.

Tozan Ryokai attained enlightenment many times. Once when he was crossing a river he saw himself reflected in the water and composed a verse, "Don't try to figure out who you are. If you try to figure out who you are, what you understand will be far away from you. You will have just an image of yourself." Actually, you are in the river. You may say that is just a shadow or a reflection of yourself, but if you look carefully with warm-hearted feeling, that is you.

You may think you are very warm-hearted, but when you try to understand how warm, you cannot actually measure. Yet when you see yourself with a warm feeling in the mirror or the water, that is actually you. And whatever you do, you are there.

When you do something with a warm-hearted feeling, Manjushri, the Bodhisattva of wisdom, is there, and there is the true you. You don't have to wonder where Manjushri is or what he is doing. When you do things with your warm-hearted mind, that is actual practice. That is how to take care of things, that is how to communicate with people.

Some of you are priests and some are not priests, and each of you will go your own way. Those of you who are not married and those of you who are married each have your own way of extending practice to your everyday lives. Although our situations are different, practice is the same, and we all meet Manjushri. Even though he is one, he is everywhere, with everyone and everything. Whatever you do, whatever your practice is, Manjushri is there. The secret is not to forget the true mercy of Buddha who takes care of everything. If we lose this point, whatever we do doesn't make sense.

So we put emphasis on warm heart, warm zazen. The warm feeling we have in our practice is, in other words, enlightenment, or Buddha's mercy, Buddha's mind. It is not a matter of just counting your breath or following your breath. If counting the breath is tedious, it may be better just to follow the breath. But the point is, while inhaling and exhaling, to take care of the breath, just as a mother watches her baby. If a baby smiles, its mother will smile. If a baby cries, its mother is worried. That kind of close relationship, being one with your practice, is the point. I am not talking about anything new—the same old things!

Our monastic rules are based on kind, warm-hearted mind. The idea is not to restrict your freedom, but rather to give you freedom to behave and act in your own way. It is not so important to follow the rules literally. Actually, if you break a rule now and then, we will know what is wrong with you, and your teacher, without criticizing you, may be able to help you more accurately. This is how to improve your practice in order to have good control over your desires and your everyday life. Then you will have big freedom from everything. That is the goal of our practice both for priests and for laypeople.

Please take care of your practice. Be very kind with yourself. Thank you very much.

Respect for Things

"Instead of respecting things, we want to use them for ourselves, and if it is difficult to use them, we want to conquer them."

In our zazen practice we stop our thinking, and we are free from our emotional activity. We don't say there is no emotional activity, but we are free from it. We don't say we have no thinking, but our life activity is not limited by our thinking mind. In short, we can say that we trust ourselves completely, without thinking, without feeling, without discriminating between good and bad, right and wrong. Because we respect ourselves, because we put faith in our life, we sit. That is our practice.

When our life is based on respect and complete trust, it will be completely peaceful. Our relationship with nature should also be like this. We should respect everything, and we can practice respecting things in the way we relate with them.

This morning when we were bowing in the zendo, we heard a big noise overhead because upstairs in the dining room people were pushing chairs across the tile floor without picking them up. This is not the way to treat chairs, not only because it may disturb the people who are bowing in the zendo underneath, but also because fundamentally this is not a respectful way to treat things.

To push the chairs across the floor is very convenient, but it will give us a lazy feeling. Of course this kind of laziness is part of our culture, and it eventually causes us to fight with each other. Instead of respecting things, we want to use them for ourselves, and if it is difficult to use them, we want to conquer them. This kind of idea does not accord with the spirit of practice.

In the same way my teacher Kishizawa Ian did not allow us to put away the *amado* more than one at a time. Do you know the *amado?* They are the wooden doors outside of *shoji* screens, which are put up to protect the shoji from storms. At the end of the building there is a big box for storing the *amado.* Since they are sliding doors, one priest can easily push five or six doors, and another priest can wait and put them in the box. But my teacher didn't like this. He told us to move them one by one. So we would slide each door and put it in the box, one door at a time.

When we pick up the chairs one by one carefully, without making much noise, then we will have the feeling of practice in the dining room. We will not make much noise of course, but also the feeling is quite different. When we practice this way we ourselves are Buddha, and we respect ourselves. To care for the chairs means our practice goes beyond the zendo.

If we think it is easy to practice because we have a beautiful building, that is a mistake. Actually it may be quite difficult to practice with a strong spirit in this kind of setting—where we have a handsome Buddha and offer beautiful flowers to decorate our Buddha hall. We Zen Buddhists have a saying that with a blade of grass we create a golden Buddha which is sixteen feet high. That is our spirit, so we need to practice respect for things.

I don't mean that we should accumulate many leaves or grasses to make a big statue, but until we can see a big Buddha in a small leaf, we need to make much more effort. How much effort I don't know. Some people may find it quite easy, but for someone like me great effort is needed. Although seeing a large golden Buddha in a large golden Buddha is easier, when you see a large

Buddha in a blade of grass, your joy will be something special. So we need to practice respect with great effort.

In this zendo everyone can come and practice our way, experienced students and also those who don't know anything about Zen. Both will have difficulties. New students will have difficulties that they could never have imagined. Old students have a double duty to do their own practice and to encourage those who have just come. Without telling them, "you should do this" or "you shouldn't do that," the old students should lead the new students so that they can practice our way more easily.

Even though newer students don't know what Buddhism is, they will naturally have a good feeling when they come to a beautiful Buddha hall. That is the ornament of a Buddha land, but for Zen Buddhists especially, the true ornament of the Buddha hall is the people who are practicing there. Each one of us should be a beautiful flower and each one of us should be Buddha, leading people in our practice. Whatever we do, we are considering how to do this. Since there are no special rules for how to treat things or how to be friendly with others, we keep studying what will help people practice together. If you don't forget this point you will find out how to treat people, how to treat things, and how to treat yourself.

This is what we call the Bodhisattva way. Our practice is to help people, and to help people we find out how to practice our way on each moment. To stop our thinking and to be free from emotional activity when we sit is not just a matter of concentration. This is to rely completely on ourselves, to find absolute refuge in our practice. We are just like a baby who is in the lap of its mother.

I think we have a very good spirit here in this zendo. I am rather amazed at the spirit, but the next question is how to extend this spirit to your everyday life. You do it by respecting things and respecting each other, because when we respect things we will find their true life. When we respect plants we will find their real life, the power and beauty of flowers.

Though love is important, if it is separated from respect and sincerity, it will not work. With big mind and with pure sincerity and respect, love can really be love. So let's try hard and find out how to make a blade of grass into a big Buddha.

Thank you very much.

Observing the Precepts

"When you observe the precepts without trying to observe the precepts, that is true observation of the precepts."

In the full lotus position we cross the right leg over the left and the left leg over the right. Symbolically, the right is activity and the left is the opposite, calmness of mind. If the left is wisdom, the right is practice; and when we cross our legs, we don't know which is which. So even though we have two, symbolically we have oneness. Our posture is vertical without leaning right or left, backward or forward. This is an expression of perfect understanding of the teaching that is beyond duality.

When we extend this, we naturally have precepts and the study of how to observe our precepts. This posture of zazen is not just a kind of training, but is the actual way of transmitting Buddha's teaching to us. Words by themselves are not good enough to actualize his teaching, so it is transmitted through activity or through human relationship.

In addition to precepts we have the relationship between teacher and disciple. The disciple must choose the teacher, and then the teacher will accept the disciple, although sometimes a teacher may recommend another teacher. Between teachers there should not be any conflict, so if a teacher thinks another is more qualified, he may recommend him or her.

Once you become a disciple, devote yourself to studying the Way. At first as a disciple you may wish to practice with a teacher not because you want to study Buddhism but for some other reason. Still it doesn't matter, you know. If you devote yourself completely to your teacher, you will understand. You will be your teacher's disciple, and you can transmit our way. This relationship between teacher and disciple is very important, and at the same time it is difficult for both teacher and disciple to be teacher and disciple in its true sense, so they should both make their best effort.

Teacher and disciple practice various rituals together. Rituals are more than just training. Through rituals we communicate and transmit the teaching in a true sense. We put emphasis on selflessness. When we practice together, we forget our own practice. It is each individual's practice, yet it is also others' practice. For instance, when we practice chanting, we say, "Recite the sutra with your ears." Then with our ears we listen to others, while with our mouths we practice our own practice. Here we have complete egolessness in its true sense.

Egolessness does not mean to give up your own individual practice. True egolessness has forgotten egolessness. As long as you believe, "My practice is egoless," that means you stick to ego, because you stick to giving up ego-centered practice. When you practice your own practice together with others, then true egolessness happens. That egolessness is not just egolessness. It also includes ego practice, but at the same time it is the practice of egolessness that is beyond ego or egolessness. Do you understand?

This is also true in the observation of precepts. If you try to observe the precepts, that is not true observation of precepts. When you observe the precepts without trying to observe the precepts, that is true observation of the precepts. Our inmost nature can help us. When we understand the precepts as an expression of our inmost nature, that is the Way *as it is.* Then there are no precepts. When we are expressing our inmost nature, no precepts are necessary, so we are not observing any precepts. On the other hand we have the opposite nature, so we want to observe our precepts. We feel that the necessity of observing the precepts will help us, and when we understand the precepts in this negative or prohibitory sense that is also the blossoming of our true nature. So we have a choice of how to observe precepts, one negative and the other positive. Also, when we do not feel that we can observe all the precepts, then we can choose the ones that we feel we can work with.

Precepts are not rules set up by someone. Since our life is the expression of our true nature, if something is wrong with that expression, then Buddha will say that is not the way. Then you will have precepts. The actual event or fact is first, not the rules. So it is the nature of precepts that we have a chance to choose our precepts. If you go one way, you will have these precepts; and if you take another way, you will have some other precepts. Whether you go this way or that way is up to you. Either way you will have some precepts. At first you should depend on your teacher. This is the best way, and you begin by following the prohibitory precepts. When you become familiar with our way, you will have a more positive observation of the precepts.

How a teacher points out the student's mistake is very important. If a teacher thinks that what his student did is a mistake, he is not a true teacher. It may be a mistake, but on the other hand it is an expression of the student's true nature. When we understand this, we have respect for our student's true nature, and we will be careful how we point out mistakes.

In the scriptures five points are made about how to be careful. One is that the teacher has to choose his opportunity and not point out the student's mistake in front of many people. If possible the teacher points out the mistake personally in an appropriate time and place. Secondly the teacher is reminded to be truthful, which means the teacher does not point out his disciple's mistake just because he thinks it is a mistake. When the teacher understands why the disciple did so, then he can be truthful.

The third reminder is for the teacher to be gentle and calm, and speak in a low voice rather than shouting. This is something very delicate like truthfulness, but here the scripture puts emphasis on having a calm gentle attitude when talking about someone's mistake.

The fourth one is that the teacher gives advice or points out the disciple's mistake solely for the sake of helping him, and does not do this just to get something off his chest. Here the teacher is very careful, noticing when the student is making some excuse for what he did, or when the student is not serious enough. Then the teacher should ignore him until he becomes more serious. Even though we give advice only for the sake of helping the student, still this does not mean to always be easy with the student. Sometimes we should be very tough with the student, or we cannot help in a true sense.

The last one is to point out the student's mistake with compassion, which means that the teacher is not just the teacher but also the disciple's friend. As a friend the teacher points out some problem or gives some advice.

So it is not easy to be a teacher or to be a student, and we cannot rely on anything, even the precepts. We have to make our utmost effort to help each other. And we do not observe our precepts just for the sake of precepts or practice rituals for the perfection of rituals. We are studying how to express our true nature.

Thank you very much.

Pure Silk, Sharp Iron

"We refine silk by washing it many times so that the threads are white and soft enough to weave. . . . We temper iron by hitting it while it is hot—not to forge or to shape it, but to make it strong."

Last week one of the Sunday School children saw me sitting zazen, and she said, "I can do it." She crossed her legs and said, "Now what? Now what?" I was very interested in her question because many of you have the same question. You come here every day to practice Zen, and you ask me, "Now what? Now what?"

I don't think I can fully explain this point. It is not a question that can be answered. You should know for yourself. We sit in a formal posture so we can experience something through our bodies, not by my teaching, but by your own physical practice. However, to be able to sit in a particular way and to attain a particular state of mind is not perfect study. After you have full experience of mind and body, you will be able to express it in other ways as well.

Without sticking to a formal posture, you naturally convey your mind to others in various ways. You will have the same state of mind sitting in a chair or standing, working or speaking. It is the state of mind in which you do not stick to anything. This is the purpose of our practice.

Yesterday a Japanese visitor was speaking about Japanese literature. Japanese people have been studying Chinese characters and Chinese culture since about 600 or 700 A.D., and after using Chinese characters they established their own way of writing. The same thing will happen here with our practice. One hundred years after the Japanese government stopped sending students to China to study Chinese culture, we had an exquisite Japanese culture. In the Fujiwara period especially, we had beautiful Japanese literature and calligraphy. There was a lot of freedom. Artists and scholars studied the arts, philosophy, and religion. They tried various disciplines, and they had good teachers.

The work that followed the Fujiwara period was not so good. According to my visitor some of the later calligraphy was too formal and shows too much of the artist's ego. We cannot see any personality in their calligraphy. The personality we see in art should be well trained without much ego in it. I think you can understand the difference between personality and ego. Ego is something that covers your good personality. Everyone has character, but if you don't train yourself, your character is covered by ego. You cannot appreciate your personality.

Through long practice and training, we get rid of ego. A word in Japanese that expresses this training is *neru*. *Neru* is how we refine silk by washing it many times so that the threads are white and soft enough to weave. We also use the character for iron. We temper iron by hitting it while it is hot—not to forge or to shape it but to make it strong. Hitting it after it is cold doesn't work. Training is something like this. When you are young, you have a lot of ego, a lot of desires. Through training you rub and wash your ego, and you become quite soft, like pure white silk. Even though you have strong desires, if you temper them enough, you will have strong sharp iron, like a Japanese sword. This is how we train ourselves.

This is not something for me to talk about, but something I must show you by my everyday life, which is not so good. I am afraid you will study only my weak points. We should know why we practice zazen, and we should be able to tell the difference between something that is good and something that just looks good. There is a big difference.

Unless you train yourself through hard practice, you will have no eyes to see and no feeling to appreciate something that is truly good. Only when many people have the eyes to see or to feel something good will we have good teachers and students. This is mutual practice. Buddha was great because people were great. When people are not ready, there will be no Buddha. I don't expect every one of you to be a great teacher, but we must have eyes to see what is good and what is not so good. This mind will be acquired by practice.

Even in the Fujiwara period, Chinese culture and calligraphy were far superior to Japanese. The Chinese people had various brushes and always used the brush more than the Japanese people did. The Japanese had fewer materials to make brushes. We had lots of bamboo but few sheep or animals from which to make brushes. So our training in calligraphy was more limited than that of Chinese peoples. But even before Japanese people mastered Chinese calligraphy completely, they had already started a unique Japanese calligraphy. I find this very interesting.

Historically Buddhists have been very sincere about this point. That is why we have Dharma transmission. Chinese masters especially put strong emphasis on transmission. It is necessary to master the teacher's way completely, before you are free from it. That is very hard practice. That is why it takes such a long time to be a Zen master. It is not knowledge; it is not some power. The point is whether a person is trained enough to be like pure white silk and very sharp iron. At that time, without trying to do anything, you will be able to express your personality in its true sense. If we cannot see any true personality in a person's work, it means that he has not yet eliminated his habitual way.

My own habit is absentmindedness. I am naturally very forgetful. Even though I started working on it when I went to my teacher at the age of thirteen, I have not been able to do anything about it. It is not because of old age that I am forgetful; it is my tendency. But working on it, I found that I could get rid of my selfish way of doing things. If the purpose of practice and training was just to correct your weak points, I think it would be almost impossible to succeed. Even so, it is necessary to work on them, because as you work on them, your character will be trained, and you will become free of ego.

People say I am very patient, but actually I have a very impatient character. My inborn character is very impatient. I don't try to correct it any longer, but I don't think my effort was in vain, because I studied many things. I had to be very patient in order to work on my habit, and I must be very patient when people criticize me about my forgetfulness. "Oh, he is so forgetful, we cannot rely on him at all. What should we do with him?"

My teacher scolded me every day: "This forgetful boy!" But I just wanted to stay with him. I didn't want to leave him. I was very patient with whatever he said. So I think that is why I am very patient with others' criticism about me. Whatever they say, I don't mind so much. I am not so angry with them. If you know how important it is to train yourself in this way, I think you will understand what Buddhism is. This is the most important point in our practice.

Thank you very much.

Not Always So

"This is the secret of the teaching. It may be so, but it is not always so. Without being caught by words or rules, without many preconceived ideas, we actually do something, and doing something, we apply our teaching."

Not Always So

"Real freedom is to not feel limited when wearing this Zen robe, this troublesome formal robe. Similarly in our busy life we should wear this civilization without being bothered by it, without ignoring it, without being caught by it."

In Buddhist scripture there is a famous passage that explains that water is not just water. For human beings water is water, but for celestial beings it is a jewel. For fish it is their home, and for people in hell or hungry ghosts it is blood, or maybe fire. If they want to drink it, water changes into fire, and they cannot drink it. The same water looks very different to various beings.

Most people think that "water is water" is the right understanding, and that it should not be a home or a jewel, blood or fire. Water should be water. But Dogen Zenji says: "Even though you say 'water is water,' it is not quite right."

When we practice zazen, we may think, "This is the right practice, and we will attain something correct and perfect." But if you ask Dogen Zenji, he may say, "Not quite right." This point is a good koan for you to study.

When we say, "Water is water," we understand things materially. We say that water is H_2O, but under some conditions H_2O may be ice or mist, or it may be vapor or a human body. It is only water under some circumstances. For convenience, we may tentatively say that water is water, but we should appreciate water in its true sense. Water is more than just water.

When I am drinking water, water is everything. The whole world is water. Nothing exists besides water. When we drink water with this understanding and attitude, that is water, and at the same time it is more than water.

When we "just sit" in meditation, we include everything. There is nothing else, nothing but you. That is shikantaza. We become completely ourselves. We have everything, and we are fully satisfied. There is nothing to attain, so we have a sense of gratitude or joyful mind.

I think I understand why you practice zazen. Most of you are seeking something. You seek what is true and real, because you have heard so many things that you cannot believe in. You are not even seeking for what is beautiful, because you have found that something which looks beautiful may not actually be beautiful. It is just the surface of something or just an ornament. You are also aware of how people can be hypocritical. Many people who appear to be virtuous don't convey real gratitude or joyful mind, so you don't trust them.

You don't know whom to trust or what teaching to believe, so you come here looking for something. I cannot give you what you are seeking, because I myself don't believe in any particular thing. I don't say that water is water, or that water is a jewel or a house, fire or blood. As Dogen Zenji said, water is more than that. We may want to stick to righteousness, beauty, truth, or virtue, but it is not wise to seek for something like that. There is something more.

I have noticed that you like to travel. Today Alaska, the next day India and Tibet. You are seeking for something, whether it is a fire or a jewel, or something else. When you realize it is not always so, you cannot believe in those things anymore, and your way of seeking the truth will change. Otherwise you will be sticking to something.

To seek for a great teaching like Buddhism is to seek for something good. Whatever you find, you will be like a sightseer. Even though you don't travel in your car, spiritually you are sightseeing: "Oh, what a beautiful teaching. This is a really true teaching!" To be a sightseer is one of the dangers of Zen practice. Be careful! To be captivated by the teaching doesn't help at all. Don't be fooled by things, whether it is something beautiful or something that looks true. This is just playing games. You should trust Buddha, trust the Dharma, and trust the Sangha in its true sense.

Real freedom is to not feel limited when wearing this Zen robe, this troublesome formal robe. Similarly in our busy life we should wear this civilization without being bothered by it, without ignoring it, without being caught by it. Without going anywhere, without escaping it, we can find composure in this busy life.

Dogen Zenji says to be like a boatman. Although he is carried by the boat, he is also handling the boat. That is how we live in this world. Even though you understand how to live in this world like a boatman, that does not mean you are able to do it. It is very difficult, which is why you practice zazen.

Yesterday I said, "However painful your legs are, you shouldn't move," and some people may have understood what I said literally. What I was really saying is that your determination to practice zazen should be like that. If it is too painful, you can change your posture, but your determination should be like that. And "should be" is also a good example. It is not necessarily so.

The secret of Soto Zen is just two words: "Not always so." Oops—three words in English. In Japanese, two words. "Not always so." This is the secret of the teaching. It may be so, but it is not always so. Without being caught by words or rules, without too many preconceived ideas, we actually do something, and doing something, we apply our teaching.

To stick to something rigidly is laziness. Before you do something difficult, you want to understand it, so you are caught by words. When you are brave enough to accept your surroundings without saying what is right and what is wrong, then the teaching that was told to you will help. If you are caught by the teaching, you will have a double problem—whether you should follow the teaching or go your own way. This problem is created by grasping the teaching. So practice first, and then apply the teaching.

We practice zazen like someone close to dying. There is nothing to rely on, nothing to depend on. Because you are dying, you don't want anything, so you cannot be fooled by anything.

Most people are not only fooled by something, they are also fooled by themselves, by their ability, their beauty, their confidence, or their outlook. We should know whether or not we are fooling ourselves. When you are fooled by something else, the damage will not be so big, but when you are fooled by yourself, it is fatal.

You may feel some resistance to this Zen way of life or to your life in the world, but don't be lost in resistance. Do you understand? If you are deeply involved in resistance or fight, you will lose yourself. You will lose your strength, lose your friends and your parents. You will lose everything, your confidence, the brightness of your eyes. You are a dead body! And no one will say: "Oh, I am sorry." No one will say so. Look at your face in the mirror to see if you are still alive or not. Even though you practice zazen, if you don't stop being fooled, it won't help at all. Do you understand?

Let's practice hard, while we are still a little bit alive.

Thank you very much.

Direct Experience of Reality

"When you study something with your whole mind and body, you will have direct experience. When you believe you have some problem it means your practice is not good enough. When your practice is good enough, whatever you see, whatever you do, that is the direct experience of reality."

Zen Master Dogen said: "Mountains and rivers, earth and sky— everything is encouraging us to attain enlightenment." In the same way the purpose of my lecture is to encourage you to attain enlightenment, to have a real experience of Buddhism. Even though you think you are studying Buddhism when you are reading, you may have just an intellectual understanding rather than a direct experience.

Intellectual understanding is necessary, but it will not complete your study. This does not mean to ignore intellectual understanding, or that enlightenment is entirely different from intellectual understanding. The true, direct experience of things can be intellectualized, and this conceptual explanation may help you have direct experience. Both intellectual understanding and direct experience are necessary, but it is important to know the difference. Sometimes you may think something is an enlightenment experience, and it is just intellectual. That is why you must have a true teacher who knows the difference.

So when we study Buddhism, it is necessary to have strong conviction, and to study not only with our mind but also with our body. If you come to the lecture even though you are sleepy and unable to listen to it, your attending the lecture will bring you some experience of enlightenment. It will be enlightenment itself.

Direct experience will come when you are completely one with your activity; when you have no idea of self. This could be when you are sitting, but it could also be whenever your way-seeking mind is strong enough to forget your selfish desires. When you believe you have some problem it means your practice is not good enough. When your practice is good enough, whatever you see, whatever you do, that is the direct experience of reality. This point should be remembered. Usually, without knowing this point we are involved in judgments, so we say, "this is right, that is wrong," "this is perfect," and "that is not perfect." That seems ridiculous when we are doing real practice.

Sometimes we may say that for Buddhists there is nothing wrong. Whatever you do, you know, "Buddha is doing it, not me," or, "Buddha is responsible, not me." But if you use that as an excuse, that is a misunderstanding. We say, "All beings have Buddha Nature" to encourage you to have an actual experience of it. The purpose of the statement is just to encourage your true practice, not to give you some excuse for your lazy practice or your practice that is merely formal.

In China people would carry something on their heads, perhaps honey or water in big jars. Sometimes someone must have dropped the jar. This is a big mistake, of course, but if you do not look back, it is all right. You just go on and on, even though there is no more honey or water on your head. If you go on and on, that is not a mistake. But if you say, "Oh! I lost it! Oh my!" that is a mistake. That is not true practice.

When a skillful martial artist uses his sword, he should be able to cut a fly off his friend's nose without cutting his nose. To have the fear of cutting his nose is not true practice. When you do something, have a strong determination to do it! *Whoosh!* [Sound of sword cutting air.] Without any idea of skillful or not, dangerous or not, you just do it. When you do something with this kind of conviction, that is true practice. That is true enlightenment.

This strong conviction to realize your life is beyond "successful" or "not successful." Beyond any feeling of fear, you just do it. That is real practice and that is the way-seeking mind, which goes beyond the dualistic idea of good and bad, right or wrong. You just do it.

That is how we practice the Four Vows. We help people just because we wish to, not because we think we will be successful. Sentient beings are numberless, so we don't know if we can completely help all sentient beings. Yet it doesn't matter. As long as we are here, we should continue our practice of helping beings.

There is no limit to our understanding of the teaching. Whether we understand it or not, we go on trying to understand. When we study with this kind of conviction, we will meet with valuable teachings, rarely encountered even in a thousand kalpas. This absolute teaching is incomparable to any other teaching.

An incomparable teaching does not mean it is the best teaching. As Dogen Zenji says, "We do not discuss the meaning of the teaching in a comparative way but emphasize how to practice." We focus our study on how to accept the teaching and live the teaching. Whether or not our teaching is profound or lofty misses the point, which is to develop our attitude of study. This is characteristic of Zen and characteristic of true Buddhism. Rather than setting up a system of Buddhism, we put emphasis on true practice.

All the rules we have are just to make practice easier. Not to make our door narrow but to open our door to everyone. We know how difficult it is, so we set up some rules to help you practice. If there is no pole for you to climb up, it is difficult for you to experience the kind of feeling you will have when you jump off the top. If a baby has no toy, it is rather difficult to have the actual experience of a human being. The rules we have are a kind of toy to help your experience as a Buddhist. It does not mean that the toy is always necessary, but when you are young it is necessary.

So it is not necessary to always stick to the rules. What is important is to extend your way of life deeper and wider. To have a beautiful ceramic bowl is not necessary when you are ready to appreciate things. Whatever it is, things will encourage your practice. If you can enjoy your life in its true sense, then even if you injure your body, it is all right. Even if you die, it is all right. When you are encouraged by everything, and you realize everything is always helping you, then there is no difference whether you are dead or alive. It is all right. Quite all right. That is complete renunciation.

Your practice will be vigorous enough to continue forever, regardless of life or death. In this way, our enlightenment can be explained. How to practice in this way is up to you. I cannot explain your understanding of Buddhism. You should explain your way of life as a Buddhist in your own way.

My talk is just to encourage your practice. You cannot follow it exactly, but maybe it will give you some suggestion.

Thank you very much.

True Concentration

"You accept your thinking because it is already there. You cannot do anything about it. There is no need to try to get rid of it. This is not a matter of right or wrong but of how to accept frankly, with openness of mind, what you are doing."

True concentration does not mean to be concentrated on only one thing. Although we say, "do things one by one," what it means is difficult to explain. Without trying to concentrate our mind on anything, we are ready to concentrate on something. For instance, if my eyes are on one person in the zendo, it will be impossible to give my attention to others. So when I practice zazen, I'm not watching anybody. Then, if anyone moves, I can spot them.

Avalokiteshvara is the Bodhisattva of compassion. Sometimes portrayed as a man, Avalokiteshvara also appears in the form of a woman. Sometimes she has one thousand hands to help others, but if she concentrates on only one hand, then 999 hands will be of no use.

From ancient times the main point of practice has been to have a clear, calm mind—whatever you do. Even when you eat something good, your mind should be calm enough to appreciate the labor of preparing the food and the effort of making the dishes, chopsticks, bowls, and everything we use. With a serene mind we can appreciate the flavor of each vegetable, one by one. We don't add much seasoning, so we can enjoy the virtue of each vegetable. That is how we cook and how we eat food.

To know someone is to sense that person's flavor—what you feel from that person. Each one has his or her own flavor, a particular personality from which many feelings appear. To fully appreciate this personality or flavor is to have a good relationship. Then we can really be friendly. To be friendly does not mean to cling to someone or try to please them but to fully appreciate them.

To appreciate things and people, our minds need to be calm and clear. So we practice zazen or "just sitting" without any gaining idea. At this time you are you yourself. You "settle yourself on yourself." With this practice we have freedom, but it may be that the freedom you mean and the freedom Zen Buddhists mean are not the same. To attain freedom, we cross our legs, keep our posture upright, and let our eyes and ears be open to everything. This readiness or openness is important because we are liable to go to extremes and stick to something. In this way we may lose our calmness or mirrorlike mind.

Zazen practice is how we obtain calmness and clarity of mind, but we cannot do this by physically forcing something on ourselves or by creating some special state of mind. You may think that to have a mirrorlike mind is Zen practice. It is so, but if you practice zazen in order to attain that kind of mirrorlike mind, that is not the practice we mean. It has instead become the art of Zen.

The difference between the art of Zen and true Zen is that already you have true Zen without trying. When you try to do something, you lose it. You are concentrating on one hand out of one thousand hands. You lose 999 hands. That is why we say, "Just sit." It does not mean to stop your mind altogether or to be concentrated completely on your breathing, although these are a help. You may become bored when you practice counting the breath because it does not mean much to you, but then you have lost your understanding of real practice. We practice concentration or let our mind follow our breathing so that we are not involved in some complicated practice in which we lose ourselves, attempting to accomplish something.

In the art of Zen you try to be like a skillful Zen master who has great strength and good practice: "Oh, I want to be like him. I must try hard." The art of Zen is concerned with how to draw a straight line or how to control your mind. But Zen is for everyone, even if you cannot draw a straight line. If you can draw a line, just draw a line, that is Zen. For a child this is natural, and even though the line is not straight, it is beautiful. So whether or not you like the cross-legged position, or whether or not you think you can do it, if you know what zazen really is, you can do it.

The most important thing in our practice is just to follow our schedule and to do things with people. You may say this is group practice, but it is not so. Group practice is quite different, another kind of art. During the war some young people, encouraged by the militaristic mood of Japan, recited to me this line from the *Shushogi:* "To understand birth and death is the main point of practice." They said, "Even though I don't know anything about that sutra, I can die easily at the front." That is group practice. Encouraged by trumpets, guns, and war cries, it is quite easy to die.

That kind of practice is not our practice either. Although we practice with people, our goal is to practice with mountains and rivers, with trees and stones, with everything in the world, everything in the universe, and to find ourselves in this big cosmos. When we practice in this big world we know intuitively which way to go. When your surroundings give you a sign showing which way to go, even though you have no idea of following a sign, you will go in the right direction.

To practice our way is good, but you may be practicing with a mistaken idea. Still if you know, "I am making a mistake, but even so I cannot help continuing with my practice," then there is no need to worry. If you open your true eyes, and accept the you that is involved in a wrong idea of practice, that is real practice.

You accept your thinking because it is already there. You cannot do anything about it. There is no need to try to get rid of it. This is not a matter of right or wrong, but of how to accept frankly, with openness of mind, what you are doing. That is the most important point. When you practice zazen you will accept the you who is thinking about something, without trying to be free of the images you have. "Oh! Here they come." If someone is moving over there, "Oh, he is moving." And if he stops moving, your eyes remain the same. That is how your eyes will see when you are not watching anything special. In that way your practice includes everything, one thing after another, and you do not lose your calmness of mind.

The extent of this practice is limitless. With this as our base, we have real freedom. When you evaluate yourself as being good or bad, right or wrong, that is comparative value, and you lose your absolute value. When you evaluate yourself by a limitless measure, each one of you will be settled on your real self. That is enough, even though you think you need a better measurement. If you understand this point, you will know what real practice is for human beings and for everything.

Thank you very much.

Wherever I Go, I Meet Myself

"As long as you are clinging to the idea of self and trying to improve your practice or find something out, trying to create an improved, better self, then your practice has gone astray. You have no time to reach the goal."

Most of us want to know what the self is. This is a big problem. I am trying to understand why you have this problem. It seems to me that even though you try to understand who you are, it is an endless task, and you will never see your self. You say that to sit without thinking is difficult, but it will be even more difficult to try to think about your self. To reach a conclusion is almost impossible, and if you continue trying, you become crazy, and you won't know what to do with your self.

Your culture is based on ideas of self-improvement. The idea of improvement is rather scientific. In the scientific sense, improvement means that instead of going to Japan by ship, now you can go by jumbo jet. So improvement is based on comparative value, which is also the basis of our society and our economy. I understand that you are rejecting that idea of civilization, but you are not rejecting the idea of improvement. You still try to improve something. Perhaps most of you sit to improve your zazen, but Buddhists do not hold so strongly to the idea of improvement.

When you practice zazen trying to improve yourself, you may want to know yourself in a more psychological way. Psychology will tell you about certain aspects of yourself, but it will not tell you exactly who you are. It is just one of many interpretations of your mind. If you go to a psychologist or psychiatrist, you will endlessly have new information about yourself. As long as you are going, you may feel some relief. You may feel released from the burden you carry, but in Zen we understand ourselves quite differently.

Tozan, the founder of the Chinese Soto Zen School, said, "Don't try to see yourself objectively." In other words, don't try to seek for information about yourself that is the objective truth. That is information. He says that the real you is quite different from any information you have. The real you is not that kind of thing. "I go my own way. Wherever I go, I meet myself."

Tozan rejects your effort to cling to information about yourself, and says to go on alone using your own legs. Whatever people may say, you should go your own way, and at the same time you should practice with people. This is another point. It means that to meet yourself is to practice with people.

When you see someone practicing sincerely, you see yourself. If you are impressed by someone's practice, you may say, "Oh, she is doing very well." That "she" is neither she nor you—she is something more than that. What is she? After thinking for a while, you may say, "Oh, she is there and I am here." But when you were struck by her practice, that "her" is neither you nor her. When you are struck by something, that is actually the real you. Tentatively I say "you," but that you is the pure experience of our practice. As long as you are trying to improve yourself, you have a core idea of self, which is wrong practice. That is not the practice we mean.

When you empty your mind, when you give up everything

and just practice zazen with an open mind, then whatever you see you meet yourself. That is you, beyond she or he or me. As long as you are clinging to the idea of self and trying to improve your practice or discover something, trying to create an improved, better self, then your practice has gone astray. You have no time to reach the goal, so eventually you will get tired out, and you will say, "Zen is no good. I practiced zazen for ten years, but I didn't gain anything!" But if you just come here and sit with sincere students and find yourself among them, and you continue in that way, that is our practice. You can have this kind of experience wherever you are. As Tozan said, "Wherever I go, I meet myself." If he sees water, that is to see himself. To see water is enough for him, even though he cannot see himself in the water.

So the way to understand yourself is not by understanding yourself objectively or gathering information from various sources. If people say you are crazy—"Okay, I am crazy!" If people say you are a bad student, it may be so. "I am a bad student, but I am trying pretty hard." That is enough. When you sit in that way, you accept yourself and accept everything together with yourself. When you are involved in various silly problems, you sit with the problems you have. That is you at that time. When you try to get out of your problems, that is already wrong practice.

If you cling to an idea you create, like a self or an objective reality, you will be lost in the objective world that you create with your mind. You are creating things one after another, so there is no end. There may be various worlds you are creating, and to create and see many things is very interesting, but you should not be lost in your creations.

The other side of our practice is that we think and we act. We do not try to be like a stone. Everyday life is our practice. Instead of being enslaved by the thinking mind or the imagination or emotional activity, we just think in its true sense. Thinking comes to us from our true self, which includes everything. Before we think about it, trees, birds, and everything are thinking. And when they think, they groan or they sing. That is their thinking. There is no need for us to think more than that. If we see *things as it is*, thinking is already there. This kind of pure thinking is the thinking we have in our practice, so we always have freedom from ourselves too. We can see *things as it is*, and at the same time we can think about things. Because we do not cling to any particular standard for thinking, for us there is no true way and no false way.

Thank you very much.

The Boss of Everything

"Without being enslaved by it, you are able to share your practice with everything. That is how to establish yourself on yourself. You are ready to include everything. When you include everything, that is the real self."

The reason we practice zazen is to be the boss of everything. Wherever we are. But if I say so, it will create a misunderstanding: that you are the boss of everyone or everything. When you understand in that way, you exist as an idea in your mind. That is not the "you" we mean. That is a delusion because the ideas you have are not well supported by your practice, and you become enslaved by the idea of "you" and "others." When the real power of practice is supporting your understanding, then the you who is practicing our way is the boss of everything, the boss of you yourself.

That is why Buddha said to control yourself. The self you have to control is the deluded you, not the real you. You have an idea of who you are, and you are caught by it. You are enslaved by the deluded you, so you have difficulty or confusion. When these ideas are well controlled by the power of your practice, then that "you" is the boss of everything. Then even a confused mind will be supported by your practice.

Sounds come to your ears when you are practicing zazen. You

may hear various voices, and sometimes you may have various ideas in your mind, but if your practice is good, your practice owns or includes the things you hear and the images you have. They are a part of you. Your practice is strong enough to have them, to own them without being enslaved by them, as you have your own hands and eyes.

Sometimes it looks like the left hand and the right hand are not cooperating when you are holding something, but they are trying to do something. When you are really the boss of everything, even though it looks like confusion, it is not confusion. It may look like you are doing something wrong, and people may say, "Oh, he is doing something wrong," but that is their understanding. You are not doing anything wrong because you own everything, and you are managing things as you manage your own hands.

You are letting yourself be with everything and letting things be as they want to be. That is the power of practice, and that is quite different from doing something wrong. Someone doing something wrong may suffer, but for you there is no suffering. You are just managing things in some way, as your own.

The precepts also should be observed in this way. You observe precepts not because you have to follow Buddha's words, but to extend true practice into your everyday life or to settle yourself on yourself. That self includes everything. Sometimes we say that to extend your practice into everyday life is to be completely involved in your activity, or to be one with things, but that is not so clear. Then you may say that being caught up with baseball mania or infatuated with gambling is the same as practice, but that is not practice, because you are enslaved by it. You are not the boss of gambling—gambling is the boss of you. Your practice is not working. You are enslaved by something which you create in your mind.

Your mind whirls on and creates some delusion. You have a gaining idea or a playful speculative idea, that's all. So you are enslaved by yourself and by gambling. You are not practicing zazen at all. You are not the boss, you do not own your mind, and you do not even own your legs, because as soon as you get up, your legs want to go to Reno! Your practice does not support your legs. That is the difference.

So to be one with something does not mean to be caught by it. You are caught when you become a member of something in your mind. You create something interesting in your mind, you become very suggestible and feel the zeal to be a member of the group you have in your mind. You are enslaved by it, even though you have nothing besides what you created in your mind. There is no practice — nothing which is supporting you. You are not the boss, and you even lose yourself. That is the difference.

So we say to practice zazen without any gaining idea, without any purpose. Let things work as they do, supporting everything as your own. Real practice has orientation or direction, but it has no purpose or gaining idea, so it can include everything that comes. Whether it is good or bad doesn't matter. If something bad comes: "Okay, you are a part of me;" and if something good comes: "Oh, okay." Because we do not have any special goal or purpose of practice, it doesn't matter what comes.

Since it includes everything, we call it big mind. Whatever it is, it is included within us, and we own it, so we call it big mind or "purposeless purpose" or "tongueless tongue." Even though I talk about something, there is no purpose. I am talking to myself because you are a part of me, so I have no purpose in my talk. Something is going, that is all. It goes because of the real joy of sharing your practice with everything.

When you practice zazen, everything practices zazen, everything you have is practicing zazen. Buddha practices zazen, Bodhidharma practices zazen, and everything practices zazen with you. And you share the practice with everything. Zazen happens in that way, our real life happens in that way, our real Bodhisattva way happens in that way.

That is how you help others. To help others means to share your practice with people. We share our practice with children and with people on the street. Even though they do not practice zazen, we can share the practice, because if I see people, they are already here, and I practice zazen with them, with the sound of the car, with everything.

If someone asks me why I practice, I may answer that it is to have a well-oriented mind. The point is not to lose this well-oriented mind. In Japan children have a Bodhidharma toy. Do you know the toy? It is made of paper, and even though you push it down, it will stand back up. That is well-oriented practice. People enjoy tossing the toy around, because wherever it goes, it will stand back up. That is a good example of our practice.

We cannot find where the self is. If you say, "Here is my mind," that is already an idea of self. It is here instead of there. You think your mind is in your head, but where is it? No one knows. So our practice is to be with everything. Without being enslaved by it, you are able to share your practice with everything. That is how to establish yourself on yourself. You are ready to include everything. When you include everything, that is the real self.

Thank you very much.

Sincere Practice

"What is important is not the teaching but the character or effort of the student. Even to seek for enlightenment means your mind is not big enough. You are not sincere enough because you have some purpose in your study."

Although Dogen Zenji is considered to be the founder of the Soto Zen school in Japan, he didn't like to identify himself as "Zen," let alone "Soto." If necessary, he said to call us Buddha's disciples, and he called himself Monk Dogen.

When Dogen Zenji studied in China with the Zen master Tendo Nyojo Zenji, there were various schools of Zen like Rinzai, Soto, Ummon, Hogen, and Igyo. According to Dogen though, Nyojo Zenji did not belong to any particular school. His Zen was just to practice zazen and to realize Buddha's spirit with his own body and mind. That was why Dogen accepted him as his teacher.

In Japan Dogen had studied Tendai Buddhism and later went to Eisai Zenji's temple to study Rinzai. But Eisai died shortly after, and Dogen wanted to continue his practice with the right teacher, so he went to China with Myozen, who was one of Eisai's disciples. Although he visited many temples and saw many Zen teachers, he couldn't accept anyone as his teacher until he met Nyojo Zenji.

When Dogen Zenji saw Nyojo Zenji for the first time, even without studying under him, he accepted him as his teacher. And similarly Nyojo Zenji right away thought, "This is my disciple, who will carry on my practice." One evening during meditation, Nyojo Zenji was scolding someone who was sleeping, and at that time Dogen Zenji had an awakening. Submitting his realization to his teacher, Dogen Zenji received Dharma transmission from Nyojo Zenji. Later he returned to Japan.

The first thing we notice here is that Dogen Zenji was a monk who wanted to be a sincere disciple of the Buddha. That's all. He already had given up the scholarly study of Buddhism, so his problem was how to be a good disciple from the bottom of his heart and mind. To have this spirit is the most important point. Since he was such a sincere student, he could not accept teachers who were not as sincere as he was, and he could not accept someone who was only a good speaker. He wanted to meet a monk who was really practicing Zen in its true sense. So when he saw Nyojo Zenji, he accepted him as a teacher, and when Nyojo Zenji saw him, he acknowledged Dogen's sincerity.

What is sincere practice? When you are not so sincere it is difficult to know, but when you are sincere you cannot accept what is superficial. Only when you become very sincere will you know what it is. It is like appreciating good art. If you want to appreciate good art the most important thing is to see good work. If you have seen a lot of good work, then when you see something that is not so good you will immediately know that it is not so good. Your eyes have become sharp enough to see.

That is why Dogen Zenji put emphasis on the teacher. If you want to know what is sincerity, you should have a good teacher, because by seeing him you will know what a good teacher is. When you see a sincere person you will know what sincerity is. It is not something that I can describe. You will feel it with your intuition. That kind of intuition will be gained by seeing a good teacher.

To develop your well-polished eye, or clear, unbiased judgment, it is important to give up, or be ready to give up everything, including your understanding of the teaching and your knowledge of Buddhism. Then you will be able to tell what is good and what is bad. Many teachers gave up sutra study and only practiced zazen. They did not rely on anything, but just practiced zazen to purify their minds. Any teaching can be a good teaching for you, but because of your faulty judgment, the teaching does not make much sense. You spoil good teaching with your own judgment, but when you do not judge it, then you can accept the teaching as it is.

The teaching that Dogen received from Nyojo was this great spirit, ready to give up everything. Especially when he practiced zazen, he had nothing in his mind. That purity of practice struck him. When you are trying to give up everything, you haven't given up everything yet. When you become tired of foolish discussion or foolish study, of foolish mind grasping for something to rely on, then you will seek for something called truth or true teaching. You will be completely involved in pure practice, giving up everything.

My teacher, Kishizawa Roshi, was a great scholar, and his study started after he gave up everything. He didn't care for position, fame, or reputation. Whatever people said about him, he didn't mind. He continued his study and practice just to meet ancient teachers who had devoted themselves to the teaching. When you give up everything, there is no Soto or Rinzai. That was true with my teacher.

Whenever he met a student or scholar, he would ask for any written teachings they might have. Whatever it was, he was very much interested in reading it. He was always seeking for his friend, seeking for his teacher. It did not matter to him whether or not the person was famous. Only when you give up everything can you see the true teacher.

Even the name of Buddhism is already a dirty spot on our practice. What is important is not the teaching, but the character or effort of the student. Even to seek for enlightenment means your mind is not big enough. You are not sincere enough because you have some purpose in your study. And the desire to accomplish something or even to propagate Buddhism is not pure enough. Just to see someone who is holy, great, and pure is the purpose of our study of Zen or Buddhism.

On that point your teacher should be strict. When you are lazy he will be very angry. If you are always involved in something that is not pure enough, you are wasting your time. As much as possible, follow your inner voice, rejecting useless things. Dogen Zenji said that if your practice is pure enough you will be supported by Buddha, so do not worry about who will support you or what will happen to you. Moment after moment completely devote yourself and listen to your inner voice. Then you will see someone who is great in the true sense. You will see someone who can accept you, someone whom you can accept. That is the most important point for Zen students. If you cannot accept your teacher in this way, seek for someone else. Without this kind of spirit it is almost impossible to study our way.

To realize way-seeking mind is to practice zazen, and how you practice zazen is to have the right posture. Tatsugami Roshi mentioned an interesting way to practice right posture by saying, "Yes." That was very good! How about my mudra? "Yes." How about my eyes? "Yes." In short, zazen is "Yes." My spine— "Yes." My chin—"Yes." You are not actually checking your posture. You are just accepting your posture—"Yes."

That is zazen. There is no extra activity in your practice; that is the spirit for you to have. There is no other secret in our practice. If you have something more than that, it is heresy. When you have some extra fancy practice, you will not reach this point.

It is the same thing with the precepts, such as "Don't kill." You may think that you cannot survive if you do not kill anything. But whether or not it is possible is out of the question. If the precept says, "Don't kill," then you say, "Yes, I will not kill." At that time you have perfect Buddha nature. When you say it is not possible, it is right or wrong, or you compare Buddhist precepts to Christian commandments, you lose the point. When you say, "Okay," whether to the commandments or the precepts, there we have Buddha mind or perfect mercy. So if you notice this point there is no other secret. When you listen to your inner voice directly, without even trying to listen to it, whenever you have a chance to hear it, there is the Way. There is the voice of Buddha.

Thank you very much.

One with Everything

". . . Wherever you are, you are one with the clouds and one with the sun and the stars that you see. Even if you jump out of the airplane, you don't go anywhere else. You are still one with everything. That is more true than I can say and more true than you can hear."

Most of us understand things in terms of differences such as big or small, black or white, material or spiritual. When we say spiritual, we mean something that is not material, but according to Buddhism, what is spiritual still belongs to the phenomenal side of reality. The other side, what we might call the ontological or noumenal side, is what you cannot see. Before "spiritual" or "material," the other side is already there. It is not something that can be understood by your small mind in terms of big or small, black or white, man or woman. To understand only in this way is to put a limitation on our actual being.

As long as you are trying to understand reality or you yourself in phenomenal terms it is not possible. When you understand that there is something more than spiritual or material, more than right or wrong, that is reality. That is actually each one of us. To know this is to have renunciation, to be free from ideas of right or wrong, life or death, spiritual or material.

Though you try very hard to be spiritual, still you are existing only on one side, ignoring the other side of yourself. That is why you suffer. If you really want to attain enlightenment and realize the real you, you have to go beyond ideas of good or bad, life or death. How we do this is through zazen. If something comes, let it come. Don't think about it in terms of good or bad. Let it come and let it go. That is actually zazen—to go beyond various ideas and just be yourself.

You and others are not just spiritual or physical. Even though a person appears to be doing something wrong, who can say for sure? People may say so or you may say so, but that person is not good or bad. Society has a standard. Tentatively we have a moral code, and we say this is good and this is bad. But it may change. If the moral code or standard of judging changes, then someone who is bad today can be good tomorrow or in one or two years. Good and bad are up to the times; but things themselves—things themselves are not good or bad.

How things go is a matter of cause and effect. Things that exist now will cause some effect, and that effect will cause another effect. Something that is not good and not bad is going in that way. That is reality. Not realizing this point, you tend to understand things in terms of good or bad; you think there is a good person and a bad person. But I don't understand in that way. Things are just going on. If we realize this point, that is renunciation.

When you sit in zazen, you are you. You cannot say, "I am a good person. My practice is perfect." Of course you are perfect —from the beginning. But it is not necessary for you to say that you are perfect. You are perfect even though you don't realize you are perfect. That is why we say we are all Buddha and our Buddha nature is constantly developing.

We say that I am here and you are there. It is okay to say so, but actually without me you don't exist. Without you I don't exist. This is very true. Since I am here, you are there. Since you are there, I am here. You may say that even though I don't come to Tassajara, you exist here waiting for me. Maybe so, but that is not perfect understanding. I have been at 300 Page Street, which is related to everything, and you are also related to everything. I couldn't say good-bye to the building that is related to the freeway, trees, air, stars, moon, and sun. If I am related to the sun and moon as you are related to the sun and moon, then how is it possible to say that I am here and you are there when we are always related?

It is just your mind that says you are here and I am there, that's all. Originally we are one with everything. If someone dies you may say he is no more, but is it possible for something to vanish completely? That is not possible, and it is not possible for something to appear all of a sudden from nothing. Something that is here cannot vanish completely. It can change its form, that's all. So we are always one.

Superficially you may say you are feeling lonely, but if you are very sincere and really give up your small mind, then there is no fear and no emotional problem. Your mind is always calm, your eyes are always open, and you can hear the birds as they sing. You can see the flowers as they open. There is nothing for you to worry about. And if you worry, you will see it as an interesting novel. To read it is very interesting, but it is not something to fear or worry about. We can enjoy our life fully when we understand things in that way.

When I was flying back from the East Coast the other day, I saw a beautiful sunset. The sunset lasts a pretty long time if you are flying towards the west. People on the ground think it is dark and there is no more sun, but if you are flying high up in the sky you still have the sunset, and you can see beautiful clouds. It is wonderful to see, but at the same time someone may feel very lonely. Yet wherever you are, you are one with the clouds and one with the sun and the stars that you see. Even if you jump out of the airplane, you don't go anywhere else. You are still one with everything. That is more true than I can say, and more true than you can hear.

I am not talking about something that is strange or mystical. If you think so, it means that you are not truthful enough. You are not feeling deeply enough to feel what is true. Be sincere enough to be yourself. That is the direction of our effort. Again, Dogen said that if you want to attain renunciation from birth and death, don't try to get out of birth and death. Birth and death are our equipment for this life. Without birth and death we cannot survive. It is our pleasure to have birth and death. That is how we understand truth.

In short don't be involved in making too many homemade cookies, your ideas of big or small, good or bad. Make only as many as you need. Without food you cannot survive, so it is good to make cookies, but don't make too many. It is good to have problems, and without problems we cannot survive, but not too many. You don't need to create more problems for yourself; you have enough problems.

If you really understand your life, it is not even necessary to practice zazen or even for me to come and stay in America. If you could make just enough homemade cookies for yourself, it would be okay for me to go back to Japan and eat Japanese cookies. Since you make too many cookies, I have to eat some. I have to help you. If we realize this point and enjoy just enough homemade cookies, that is the Buddhist way. That is how to enjoy life and that is why we practice zazen. We do not practice zazen to attain special enlightenment. Just to be ourselves and just to be free from our useless efforts or tendencies, we practice zazen.

Thank you very much.

Wherever You Are, Enlightenment is There

"Even in our imperfect practice, enlightenment is there. We just don't know it. So the point is to find the true meaning of practice before we attain enlightenment. Wherever you are, enlightenment is there. If you stand up right where you are, that is enlightenment."

Wherever You Are, Enlightenment is There

"Nothing we see or hear is perfect. But right there in the imperfection is perfect reality."

In our practice the most important thing is to realize that we have Buddha nature. Intellectually we may know this, but it is rather difficult to accept. Our everyday life is in the realm of good and bad, the realm of duality, while Buddha nature is found in the realm of the absolute where there is no good and no bad. There is a twofold reality. Our practice is to go beyond the realm of good and bad and to realize the absolute. It may be rather difficult to understand.

Hashimoto Roshi, a famous Zen master who passed away in 1965, said that the way we [Japanese] cook is to prepare each ingredient separately. Rice is here and pickles are over there. But when you put them in your tummy, you don't know which is which. The soup, rice, pickles, and everything get all mixed up. That is the world of the absolute. As long as rice, pickles, and soup remain separate, they are not working. You are not being nourished. That is like your intellectual understanding or book knowledge — it remains separate from your actual life.

Zazen practice is mixing the various ways we have of understanding and letting it all work together. A kerosene lamp will not work merely because it is filled with kerosene. It also needs air for combustion, and even with air, it needs matches. By the aid of matches, air, and kerosene, the lamp will work. This is our zazen practice.

In the same way, even though you say, "I have Buddha nature," that alone is not enough to make it work. If you do not have a friend or a Sangha, it won't work. When we practice with the aid of the Sangha, helped by Buddha, we can practice zazen in its true sense. We will have bright light here in the Tassajara zendo or in our daily life.

To have a so-called enlightenment experience is of course important, but what is more important is to know how to adjust the flame in zazen and in our everyday life. When the flame is in complete combustion, you don't smell the oil. When it is smoky you will smell something. You may realize that it is a kerosene lamp. When your life is in complete combustion you have no complaint, and there is no need to be aware of your practice. If we talk too much about zazen, it is already a smoky kerosene lamp.

Maybe I am a very smoky kerosene lamp. I don't necessarily want to give a lecture. I just want to live with you: moving stones, having a nice hot spring bath, and eating something good. Zen is right there. When I start to talk, it is already a smoky kerosene lamp. As long as I must give a lecture, I have to explain: "This is right practice, this is wrong, this is how to practice zazen. . . ." It is like giving you a recipe. It doesn't work. You cannot eat a recipe.

Usually a Zen master will say: "Practice zazen, then you will attain enlightenment. If you attain enlightenment you will be detached from everything, and you will see *things as it is.*" Of course this is true, but our way is not always so. We are studying how to adjust the flame of our lamp back and forth. Dogen Zenji makes this point in the *Shobogenzo*. His teaching is to live each moment in complete combustion like a lamp or a candle. To live each moment, becoming one with everything, is the point of his teaching and his practice.

Zazen practice is a very subtle thing. When you practice zazen, you become aware of things you did not notice while you were working. Today I moved stones for a while, and I didn't realize that my muscles were tired. But when I was calmly sitting zazen, I realized, "Oh! My muscles are in pretty bad condition." I felt some pain in the various parts of my body. You might think you could practice zazen much better if you had no problem, but actually some problem is necessary. It doesn't have to be a big one. Through the difficulty you have you can practice zazen. This is an especially meaningful point, which is why Dogen Zenji says, "Practice and enlightenment are one." Practice is something you do consciously, something you do with effort. There! Right there is enlightenment.

Many Zen masters missed this point while they were striving to attain perfect zazen: things that exist are imperfect. That is how everything actually exists in this world. Nothing we see or hear is perfect. But right there in the imperfection is perfect reality. It is true intellectually and also in the realm of practice. It is true on paper and true with our body.

You think that you can only establish true practice after you attain enlightenment, but it is not so. True practice is established in delusion, in frustration. If you make some mistake, that is where to establish your practice. There is no other place for you to establish your practice.

We talk about enlightenment, but in its true sense perfect enlightenment is beyond our understanding, beyond our experience. Even in our imperfect practice enlightenment is there.

We just don't know it. So the point is to find the true meaning of practice before we attain enlightenment. Wherever you are, enlightenment is there. If you stand up right where you are, that is enlightenment.

This is called I–don't-know zazen. We don't know what zazen is anymore. I don't know who I am. To find complete composure when you don't know who you are or where you are, that is to accept *things as it is*. Even though you don't know who you are, you accept yourself. That is "you" in its true sense. When you know who you are, that "you" will not be the real you. You may overestimate yourself quite easily, but when you say, "Oh, I don't know," then you are you, and you know yourself completely. That is enlightenment.

I think our teaching is very, very good, but if we become arrogant and believe in ourselves too much we will be lost. There will be no teaching, no Buddhism at all. When we find the joy of our life in our composure, we don't know what it is, we don't understand anything, then our mind is very great, very wide. Our mind is open to everything, so it is big enough to know before we know something. We are grateful even before we have something. Even before we attain enlightenment, we are happy to practice our way. Otherwise we cannot attain anything in its true sense.

Thank you very much.

Not Sticking to Enlightenment

"Real enlightenment is always with you, so there is no need for you to stick to it or even to think about it. Because it is always with you, difficulty itself is enlightenment. Your busy life itself is enlightened activity. That is true enlightenment."

Hui Neng, the Sixth Ancestor, said, "To dwell on emptiness and to keep a calm mind is not zazen." He also said, "Just to sit in a cross-legged posture is not Zen." At the same time I always say to you, "Just sit." If you don't understand what our practice is and stick to the words, you will be confused, but if you understand what real Zen is, you will know that the Ancestor's words are a kind of warning for us.

Now our sesshin is almost at an end, and soon you will be going back to your homes and becoming involved in your everyday activity. If you have been practicing true zazen, you may be happy to go back to your everyday life. You may feel encouraged to go back, but if you feel hesitant to go back to your city life or everyday life, it means that you still stick to zazen. That is why the Sixth Ancestor said, "If you dwell on emptiness, and stick to your practice, then that is not true zazen."

When you practice zazen, moment after moment, you accept what you have now, in this moment, and you are satisfied with everything you do. Because you just accept it, you don't have any complaints. That is zazen. Even if you cannot do that, you know what to do. Then sitting zazen will encourage you to do other things as well. Just as you accept your painful legs while sitting, you accept your everyday life, which may be more difficult than your zazen practice.

If you come to have a taste of real practice, especially in this seven-day sitting, and then return to your busy activity without losing the taste of practice, that will be a great encouragement. Even though it is difficult, and even though you are busy, you will always have the taste of calmness in your mind, not because you stick to it, but because you enjoy it. When you enjoy it, you don't have to stick to it. So if you have a real taste of our practice, you can enjoy it all the time, whatever you do.

You may think you have attained enlightenment, but if you are busy or in some difficulty and think you need to have that experience again, that is not real enlightenment, because it is something you are sticking to. Real enlightenment is always with you, so there is no need for you to stick to it or even to think about it. Because it is always with you, difficulty itself is enlightenment. Your busy life itself is enlightened activity. That is true enlightenment.

Nowadays young people are dating, but enlightenment is not something that you can meet on a date. If you organize your life, get up at a certain time, pick up your bag lunch at a certain time, and leave for work, then if you have a girlfriend or boyfriend, you will meet them. There is no need to make a date. At a certain time she will come to the corner where you usually see her. That is our way. It is rather foolish and troublesome to make phone calls. Even if you make a date by telephone—"Hey, I am leaving now"—if she doesn't come to the corner, you will be disappointed. If you do not make a date, and she comes to the corner, you will be really happy.

That is how you attain enlightenment. It is not a laughing matter. I am talking about something real. Not to make any date means not to expect or stick to enlightenment. When you are encouraged by enlightenment, then seeing her, even just a glimpse of her, is enough. All day long you will be happy. If you are demanding too much of her, then it already means that you stick to enlightenment.

That is what the Sixth Ancestor meant when he said, "Just to dwell on emptiness is not true practice." Originally he attained enlightenment by one famous statement: "Without dwelling on anything, you have true mind." So if you stick to something, you will lose your enlightenment. Even though you try hard to make a date or an appointment, it doesn't work. The enlightenment you attain in that way is something that you stick to, not something that is always with you, that always encourages you.

This point is very important. Even after we finish our sesshin, continue to practice in your everyday lives and have real enlightenment. This was a very fruitful sesshin, and some of you had a good taste of our practice. Even if you haven't, I think you understand how to practice zazen. So from now on just continue to practice sincerely according to the right instruction of your teacher, and someday you will have a taste of it.

Thank you very much.

The Teaching Just for You

*". . . Even though you say your practice is not good enough,
there is no other practice for you right now. Good or bad,
it is your practice."*

Usually when we practice we expect something: if we try hard, our practice will improve. If we aim at a goal in our practice, we will eventually reach it. We have the idea that our practice will improve day by day, and it will help our health and mental condition. This is true, but it is not a complete understanding.

We also do zazen with the understanding that the goal is not reached in one or two years, but is right here. Here is the goal of practice. When you practice with this understanding, you take care of many things and you remain concentrated, completely involved in the practice you have right now. That is why we have various instructions, so that you can practice hard enough to feel the goal of practice right now, as you are doing it.

You may say, "My practice is not good enough to feel the goal or the full meaning right now." But even though you say your practice is not good enough, there is no other practice for you right now. Good or bad, it is your practice. To approach perfect practice, there is no way other than to accept yourself. To say your practice is bad does not help your practice. To say your practice is excellent does not help. Your practice is your practice.

You are talking about it in various ways, good or bad, that is all. We should know this point first of all, so we say, "Even though your practice is not so good, that is perfect practice. Just sit."

Hearing this, you may understand it objectively and use it as an excuse: "Anyway, we are sitting here in the zendo, so that is perfect practice. There is no need to encourage ourselves, and there is no need to sit all day long. If we sit a little bit, that is okay, even one period is enough." That kind of understanding is very superficial. You have no understanding from your subjective side.

Truth is always here. But just to say so, when you are not actually practicing the truth, is what we call a "painted cake," a picture of a cake that you cannot eat. Even though you are sitting, you are eating a painted cake. So there is no taste, and you will give up because it doesn't mean anything: "It doesn't result in anything, so it may be better to go downtown to eat something, instead of eating the food Zen Center provides."

You may be pleased when people call you a Zen student. Then your practice is encouraging your ego, but you are not practicing Zen. When you sit like that, Zen does not mean anything. True zazen cannot be like that. If Zen were like that, it would have vanished from this world a long time ago. Zen is still alive because of the other side of the truth. Various ancestors and great sages of Buddhism have said, "Buddha left this teaching just for me, not for anyone else. Buddha left *The Lotus Sutra* just for Nichiren." If that side is forgotten, the Buddha's teaching is nothing but wastepaper. "Just for me" is not arrogance. It means you have full appreciation of the teaching as your own.

That is the spirit we need in our zazen practice. Everyone can be Nichiren; everyone can be Dogen or Bodhidharma. Because I practice zazen, there is Buddha, there is Dogen and Bodhidharma, and there is Buddha's teaching. You realize that you are the only being in this world, and that no one can take over your position. That is true—all the teaching is just for you. When you are young, you have no such feeling. You think you will live fifty or even one hundred years more, so today is not so valuable to you. If you become my age, you will really feel, "I am just this one being. No one can take over my position, so I must not fool myself."

This point is very important for everyone, but especially for those who practice our way. Without this confidence or understanding, you will expose the weakness of your practice: "Oh, no, I am not good enough. Look at me—I cannot practice zazen. Zen is so beautiful and so perfect, but it is impossible for me to do this practice." You will feel the weaknesses of your character and of your conduct, and being preoccupied in this way, you won't be able to sit. But whatever you say about yourself, you are the only one. You cannot escape, because the whole world is yours. This is beyond the truth that we can talk about. This is ultimate truth.

How can you deny the fact that you are the only one? You can criticize yourself; that is easy. But when you accept the fact that you are the only one, you have no time to say "good practice" or "bad practice." Because you turn a deaf ear to this truth, you have time to criticize yourself. When you realize this point, you can hear or see the truth, and you can practice zazen. You can accept the truth, whatever it is. To practice is to open yourself up to everything you see as an embodiment of the truth. This is why we practice zazen, why everyone can join our practice, and why this practice includes every activity in your life.

This is not a practice that can be compared to other practices as a means of attaining something. From the experiences of many people, instructions were accumulated for the forms we use and the way we breathe, just as scientific knowledge is accumulated. But Buddhist wisdom puts emphasis on the subjective side of the truth. That is why we say everyone is Buddha. That is how we transmit Buddha's teaching to everyone. It is not just a paper transmission. The subjective side has always been with us, and this point has always been emphasized without losing the objective side of the truth.

Sometimes people who call themselves "spiritual" ignore the objective side of the truth. That is also a mistake, but to be caught by the objective side of the truth and rely on it with an idle attitude will not help. Even though we can go to the moon, it doesn't help so much. As long as we rely on objective, scientific truth, it doesn't help. Only when each one of us feels the truth, appreciates, accepts, and is ready to follow the truth, will it work. When someone puts himself outside of the truth in order to study the truth, he won't know what to do when something happens to him.

In an ancient Chinese story, there was a person who liked dragons very much. He talked about dragons, he painted dragons, and he bought various kinds of dragons. So there was a dragon who thought, "If a real dragon like me visited him, he would be very happy." One day the real dragon sneaked into his room, and the man didn't know what to do! *Whaaah!* He could not even run away. He could not even stand up. For a long time we have been like the man who admired dragons, but we should not just be the dragon's friend or admirer; we should be the dragon itself. Then we will not be afraid of any dragon.

So we are ready to study our way subjectively as well as objectively. When you practice in this way, zazen will become your own zazen, and as you are Buddha, you will express your true nature in various ways. That is freedom from the forms of practice. Whatever you do, you will really be you. You will be Buddha, in its true sense. There is a big difference between prac-

tice with this understanding and lazy practice with poor, superficial understanding of form, instruction, and teaching. After all,
as Buddha said, there is no one you can rely on, so you should be
the boss of everything. Then you will understand Buddha's
teaching and our practice as your own.

Thank you very much.

Stand Up by the Ground

"The ground is not always the same. It can be a stick sometimes, or it can be a stone. It can even be water. The ground . . . means everything, not just 'ground.' It means to practice our way without trying to repeat the same experience."

When we talk about reality, it is to understand how to practice our way in zazen and in our everyday life. Dogen Zenji talked about the nature of reality by using the Chinese or Japanese word, *immo,* which can mean "like this" or "just this," but can also be a question, "What is this?"

Immo can also be "it." In English you say, "It is hot." That "it" is the same word, the same meaning as when you say, "It is nine o'clock." You use "it" for the time or the weather, but not only for the time or weather, everything is actually "it." "We" are also "it," you know, but we don't say "it." Instead of "it" we say "he" or "she," "me" or "I." But actually we mean, "it." So if everything is "it," it is at the same time a question mark. When I say "it," you won't know exactly what I mean, so you may ask, "What is 'it'?"

When we talk about time, "it" may be mealtime or lecture time. We don't know, so "it" may be a question mark for everyone. You may say, "What time is it?" or "Is it time for lecture?" So "it" or *immo* is something definite, and at the same time, a question. And this is very important for us to know. Right now "it" is hot, but "it" is not always hot. Sometime "it" will be cold.

When we talk about time, we can see that time is continuous and also that time is definite. When we say "it" is half-past eight, we point out a certain time. Now time is discontinuous. But time by its nature is continuous, so the one word has two sides: continuity and discontinuity. That is the nature of reality.

Dogen Zenji talks about practice not as something special, but something continuous, something mixed up with everything. He says: "If you fall on the ground, stand up by the ground." Does it make sense? If you fall on the ground, you stand up by the ground in that place. Also he says, "If you fall on the ground, stand up by emptiness, by nothing." Without discussing why this is so, we cannot have a complete understanding of our teaching.

Actually we stand up by the ground like this, but he says that we shouldn't. What does it mean? If you think you can always stand up by the ground, and don't mind falling on the ground, you will fall on the ground quite easily. You will have the idea: "It is all right. If I fall to the ground, I can stand up by the ground." If we practice with this kind of prejudice or easy idea, that is wrong practice.

This point is important. It is like enlightenment. If you rely on enlightenment, you will be someone who easily makes mistakes or falls on the ground, relying on the help of the ground. Do you understand? It is a very subtle point. Of course we have to stand up by the ground, but if we stick to the idea of the help of the ground all the time, we will lose the true meaning of the fall to the ground. In other words, even though we make a mistake, we should not make the same mistake many, many times, thinking it is all right because we know how to get up.

This is not what we mean when we say reality. Things do not happen twice in the same way. The ground is not always the same. It can be a stick sometimes, or it can be a stone. It can even be water. The ground is "it," you know. "It" means everything, not just "ground." It means to practice our way without trying to repeat the same experience.

So there is nothing to rely on in our practice. But on the other hand, there is always something provided for you, always. According to the circumstances, you will have some aid to practice our way. Even the pain in your legs is an aid. By the pain you have, you practice our way. The pain is "it." "It" is everything, but at that time, "it" is some definite experience or particular trouble. "It" can be drowsiness; "it" can be hunger; "it" can be hot weather. So hot weather or nice cool weather, or hunger, or mosquitoes, or the pain in your legs can be an aid to your practice with which you can stand up and establish your practice. So not only Buddha's teaching, but everything can be an aid to us.

Immo-ji means "things," and *immo-nin* is someone who is practicing zazen. "Someone practicing something"—that is reality. Or we could say, "someone doing something." Then *immo* is a discontinuous, particular being which has form and color. But as Dogen Zenji says, Zen practice is something continuous, something mixed up with everything.

If it is so, then "someone doing zazen" already includes everything. Someone cannot be separate from this world. Some action cannot exist without the background of the whole world, and some thing cannot be apart from other things. So "someone," "doing," and "something" is the same thing, you know. If they are the same thing, then we can say "something" "something" "something." What is that? That is complete realization. Everything happens in this way. So if you stick to the idea of help or enlightenment, that is already a mistake. You have separated yourself from everything.

Someone may say, "Oh, he studies Soto Zen, but he denies the enlightenment experience." It is not so. We Soto students do not stick to anything. We have complete freedom of practice, complete freedom of expression. Our practice is the living expression of our true nature or reality. So for us it is not possible to stick to anything. Moment after moment, we practice in a renewed, refreshed way.

Our practice should be independent from past practice and future practice. We cannot sacrifice our present practice for some future attainment, because all the Buddhas attained enlightenment in this way, and all the Buddhas in the future will attain enlightenment in this way. In this way means not any particular way. Sometimes it may be Soto way, sometimes Rinzai. According to the circumstances, it may be the way of another school.

Someone may attain enlightenment when he sees a flower or hears a sound. Someone may attain enlightenment when taking a hot bath or going to the rest room. Rich and poor may attain enlightenment in various ways. So actually there is not a Soto way or a Rinzai way.

We have discussed practice rather abstractly, but this is what it means: whatever it is, we should accept it. By various means moment after moment, we practice our way. There is no other way to attain enlightenment.

Thank you very much.

Just Enough Problems

"Before you accept the problems you have, the position you are in, you cannot accept yourself as you are. . . . When you are patient enough and wait until the problem makes some sense to you, you can appreciate your being here and your position, whatever it is."

This is the seventh and last day of our sesshin. We have already come this far, so we cannot give up! The only way is to stay here. I feel I have a very good crop. You may feel you are not yet ripe, but even though you are still ripening, if you stay in our store-house, you will be good apples. So I have nothing to worry about, and I don't think you have any reason to worry about your practice either.

Some of you may have started this sesshin because you had many problems. You thought that if you sat here for seven days your problems would be solved, but whatever problems you may have, they can be solved anyway. Buddha will not give you more problems than you can solve, or more than you need. Whatever the problems are, they are just enough. If these are not enough problems, Buddha is ready to give you more, just so you can appreciate your problems. Buddha is always giving you something. If you have nothing to cope with, your life feels empty. So I think you should trust Buddha. A life without problems is like sitting in this zendo for seven days without doing anything.

Here in the zendo meditating for seven days, you have had many problems. You might think you have more problems while sitting than you have in your daily life. Actually you are finding the problems you have had all along, but didn't notice because you were fooled by something. When you are not aware of your problems, they will appear unexpectedly. No problem will appear that you did not originally have, but because you overlook it, you do not expect it. So it is better to see your problems as soon as possible.

Soto students sit zazen facing the wall. Buddha is there behind you, and you are trusting him. If you trust completely, there is no need to face Buddha. This is an attitude of complete trust. Your enemies or problems will come from the back, not from the front. So to expose your back to Buddha means to express complete trust in the Buddha.

Even though you feel you have too many problems, when you trust in Buddha, you sit with your problems. At the same time, you should be ready to refuse a problem if it is too much. Buddha may say, "If you really don't need it, I will accept it at any time. Give it back to me." But more and more the problem will change into something you need. You will think, "If I refuse this problem, I may regret it. Since I am not so sure whether this is a real problem or Buddha's help, maybe it is better to keep it." If you sit in this way, you will find that your problems are valuable treasures that are indispensable for you.

Before you accept the problems you have in your position, you cannot accept yourself as you are. You cannot sit in a true way. When you steady your mind, trust Buddha, and just sit, there is no confusion or problem anymore. When you are patient enough and wait until the problem makes some sense to you, you can appreciate your being here and your position, whatever it may be. That is how you practice zazen.

When you practice zazen, there is no need to expect Buddha to help you solve your problems. Buddha is already helping you, but usually we refuse Buddha's offer. When you ask for help, you are asking for something that has not yet arrived. You are refusing to accept the treasure you already have. You are like a pig. When I was young, as my father was very poor, he raised pigs. If you give pigs a bucket of food, as long as you remain there they will not eat it, expecting you to give them more food. If you move away too quickly, they will kick over the food bucket chasing after you. So you must be very careful.

I think that is what you do. Instead of working with the problems you have, you cause yourself more problems by seeking for something else. But there is no need to seek for anything. You have plenty of problems, just enough. This is a mysterious thing, the mystery of life. We have just enough problems, not too many and not too few. So there is no need to ask anyone's help.

If you are patient enough, if you are strong enough to accept your problems, then you can sit calmly and peacefully, trusting Buddha and trusting your own being. Because you are helped, and the way you are helped is perfect, you exist here. If it is too much, you will die, and if it is too little, you will die. You are receiving just what you need. So the only way is to trust Buddha, to trust your being here. That is what we call Zen.

You may think all the Zen masters are very tough. He looks tough when you need him to be tough, but he is not so tough—he is just tough enough for you, that's all! Actually, you don't need your master, if you know how to practice zazen.

I want you just to sit and to be ready to go to the marketplace as ripe apples. Let's sit with full appreciation for our practice.

Thank you very much.

Sun-Faced Buddha,
Moon-Faced Buddha

*"The Sun-faced Buddha is good; the Moon-faced Buddha is good.
Whatever it is, that is good—all things are Buddha. And there
is no Buddha, even."*

Lately I have been sick, and because I have been practicing zazen
for many years, some people may say, "He will not catch cold or
suffer from the flu . . . but isn't it funny he stayed in bed so long?"
We may believe that zazen will make us physically strong and
mentally healthy, but a healthy mind is not just healthy in the
usual sense, and a weak body is not just a weak body. Whether it
is weak or strong, when that weakness or strength is based on
what we call truth, or Buddha nature, then that is a healthy mind
and a healthy body.

My voice may not be very good yet, but today I'm testing it.
Whether it works or not, or if I speak or not, is not a big problem. Whatever happens to us is something that should happen.
The purpose of our practice is to have this kind of complete
composure.

In the *Blue Cliff Record* there is a koan concerning Baso Doitsu.
Baso was big and physically very strong, a man of great stature.
Once when Baso was ill, the monk who took care of the temple

came to visit him and asked, "How are you doing? Are you well, or not?" And Baso said, "Sun-faced Buddha, Moon-faced Buddha."

The Sun-faced Buddha is supposed to live for one thousand eight hundred years. And the Moon-faced Buddha lives only one day and one night. When I am sick, I may be the Moon-faced Buddha. When I am healthy, I am the Sun-faced Buddha. But the Sun-faced Buddha or the Moon-faced Buddha has no special meaning. Whether I am ill or healthy, I am still practicing zazen. There is no difference. Even though I am in bed, I am Buddha. So don't worry about my health.

This is quite simple. Whatever happens to Baso, he can accept *things as it is,* but we cannot accept everything. We may accept something we think is good, but if we dislike something we won't accept it. And we compare things: "He is a true Zen master, and he is not," or, "he is a good Zen student, but I am not." That kind of understanding may be quite usual, but finally you cannot figure out which idea is reliable.

The point is to attain complete composure. Ordinary effort associated with comparative thinking will not help you. To attain enlightenment means we have complete composure in our life, without any discrimination. At the same time this does not mean to stick to the attitude of non-discrimination, because that is also a kind of discrimination.

When I was still in Japan, I had some Zen students. Some of them were very rich and influential; others were students, carpenters, or other kinds of workers. In Japan we treat some people, a mayor or a teacher, in a different way. We have a special way of speaking to them. But I always told my students, "If you are a Zen student you should forget all about your position, work, or title. Otherwise you cannot practice zazen in its true sense."

When you are sitting I say, "Don't think." "Don't think"

means not to treat things in terms of good or bad, heavy or light. Just accept *things as it is.* Even though you do not think, you may hear something; and usually the moment you hear it, your reaction is, "What could it be?" "That is a car," or "That's very noisy. Maybe it's a motorcycle."

In zazen you should just hear the big noise or the small noise, and not be bothered by it. It may seem impossible, especially for a beginner, because the moment you hear it, a reaction follows. But, if you practice zazen, if you continuously just accept *things as it is,* eventually you can do it. The way you can do it is to concentrate on your posture or your breathing.

In Japan the samurai practiced zazen to master the sword. As long as he was afraid of losing his life, he could not act with his full ability. When he was free from the idea of killing or being killed, he could just react to his enemy's activity, and win. If he tried to win, he might lose. So practicing how to act without fear, which limits your activity, is the most important thing. Although it was a matter of surviving on the battlefield, the samurai fought his fight in the zendo.

When we don't have that kind of circumstance in our everyday life, we don't feel the same necessity to practice. But our human problems are created because we make an effort to achieve something, and this limits our activity. Then we cannot achieve anything.

We should understand our everyday activity in two ways, and be able to react either way without a problem. One way is to understand dualistically—good or bad, right or wrong—and we try hard to understand things in these terms. Yet we should also be able to let go of this dualistic understanding. Then everything is one. That is the other understanding, the understanding of oneness.

So you should be able to understand or accept things in these two ways, but this is not enough. It is still dualistic. Without thinking, "This is one of two understandings," you have the freedom to move from one to the other. Then you will not be caught by your understanding. Whatever you do will be the great activity of practice.

The Sun-faced Buddha is good; the Moon-faced Buddha is good. Whatever it is, that is good—all things are Buddha. And there is no Buddha, even. When you do not understand Buddha, you will be concerned if I say there is no Buddha: "You are a priest, so how can you say there is no Buddha? Why do you chant? Why do you bow to Buddha?" There is no Buddha so we bow to Buddha. If you bow to Buddha because there is Buddha, that is not a true understanding of Buddha. Sun-faced Buddha, Moon-faced Buddha—no problem. Whether I am at Tassajara or San Francisco, no problem. Even though I die, it is all right with me, and it is all right with you. And if it is not all right, you are not a Zen student. It is *quite* all right. That is Buddha.

If I suffer while I am dying, that is suffering Buddha, and there is no confusion in it. Maybe everyone will struggle because of physical agony or spiritual agony, but that is not a problem. We should be very grateful to have a limited body like yours or mine. If you had a limitless life, it would be a great problem for you.

On my wife's favorite TV program there are some ghosts of people who lived long ago. They appear in this world, and create many problems for themselves and others. That is what happens. A human being is a human being, and we can enjoy our life only with our limited body. This limitation is vital. Without limitation nothing exists, so we should enjoy it: weak body, strong body; man or woman. The only way to enjoy our life is to enjoy the limitation that is given to us.

"Sun-faced Buddha, Moon-faced Buddha" does not mean to

be indifferent: "I don't care whether it's the Sun-faced Buddha or the Moon-faced Buddha." It means that whatever it is, we just enjoy it. This is also beyond non-attachment, because when our attachment reaches the point of non-attachment, that is real attachment. If you are attached to something, be attached to something completely. SUN-FACED BUDDHA, MOON-FACED BUDDHA! "I am here. I am right here." This kind of confidence is important. When you have this kind of confidence in yourself, in your being, you can practice true zazen beyond perfect or imperfect, good or bad.

Thank you very much.

Sitting like a Frog

"A frog is a good example of our practice. When you have been practicing for a pretty long time, you will laugh, partly at someone who is involved in the wrong idea of practice, and partly at yourself who is always sitting, without doing anything, without making much progress."

Recently on a calendar I saw one of Sengai's drawings of a frog along with Sengai's saying, "If we can become a Buddha by the practice of sitting. . . ." He doesn't say anything more, but we can imagine what the frog is thinking: "If people can become a Buddha by the practice of sitting, then I too can be a Buddha." [laughs] For those of us who have some understanding of practice, when we see someone sitting to attain enlightenment, we may think, "Oh, he is sitting like a frog."

Actually a frog's way of sitting is much better than our zazen. I always admire their practice. They never get sleepy. Their eyes are always open, and they do things intuitively in an appropriate way. When something to eat comes by, they go like this: *Gulp!* They never miss anything, they are always calm and still. I wish I could be a frog.

If you understand what Sengai is saying in his picture of a frog, you have already understood what Zen is. There is a lot of humor in his picture and a good understanding of our practice. Even though our practice is not better than a frog's, we continue to sit. When you have been practicing for a pretty long time, you will laugh, partly at someone who is involved in the wrong idea of practice, and partly at yourself who is always sitting, without doing anything, without making much progress. You will laugh at yourself. When you can laugh at yourself, there is enlightenment.

Still your zazen may be a beginner's zazen or sometimes worse than a beginner's. Sometimes I am ashamed of myself when I see a student who is practicing very well: "Oh, he is very good." I wish I could be that young again, but it is too late. Anyway, our practice cannot be better than a frog sitting, but that is okay. To see someone practicing good zazen is inspiring, not only for me, but for everyone. If your zazen is good enough to give a good impression, then your zazen is pretty good even though you don't think so. Likewise, even though you think your zazen is very good and you are proud of your enlightenment experience, if your zazen does not inspire anyone, it may be wrong practice.

When we talk about the precepts we say not to do this or not to do that, but if you are doing something good like zazen you cannot do something bad at the same time. If you continue to do something good, that is how to observe our precepts. So the point is just to sit, forgetting all about fame or profit. Just sit for the sake of zazen. That is to have real way-seeking mind, to find out your inmost desire.

The practice of way-seeking mind will sharpen your intuition. Then you will have less difficulty knowing what to choose. To make a choice you try to know what is good and what is bad, so that by comparing one thing to another you can buy or get something good. Maybe you are trying to pick out fabric from all the various colors and materials, but even though you spend two or three days you may end up getting something that is not appropriate for you. You will return to the same store. If they exchange it for something else, you are lucky.

Don't say this kind of practice is useless. It is actually the first step on our way. How to have good practice and how to buy something appropriate for yourself is the same. When you are not overly involved in it and shopping too much, then you can get something appropriate.

When you know the secret of how to use your intuitive sense, your activity will be free from various restrictions, and you will find your way in your everyday life. Until you understand why we practice zazen and what is actually true activity, intuitive activity, free from various desires and restrictions, it is difficult to figure out what is good practice. Still it is okay to continue practicing, and little by little without knowing how to acquire that kind of intuitive activity, you will get it anyway. So it is rather foolish to be involved in some hard special practice. Zazen practice is hard enough, and only through zazen practice have various teachers attained—there is no other word, so I say attained—enlightenment and become real Buddhists.

If you understand real practice, then archery or other activities can be Zen. If you don't understand how to practice archery in its true sense, then even though you practice very hard, what you acquire is just technique. It won't help you through and through. Perhaps you can hit the mark without trying, but without a bow and arrow you cannot do anything. If you understand the point of practice, then even without a bow and arrow the archery will help you. How you get that kind of power or ability is only through right practice. Dogen Zenji says that to have right practice is to have a good teacher and to receive right guidance. Otherwise you will not understand Zen.

Just to continue this right practice or fundamental practice is the most important thing.

Thank you very much.

Notes about Editing the Lectures

Several years ago the Zen Center in San Francisco invited me to work on editing Suzuki Roshi's lectures. At first I was hesitant since I do not consider that I have any unique or special understanding of Roshi's words. Eventually I did agree. I decided to trust in people's trust in me.

I began reading transcriptions of the lectures, and picked out ones which appealed to me, not especially aiming to accumulate good examples of various teachings, but to have lectures which were evocative—often focused around a particular image, whether it was that of a frog, a turtle, or an elephant; that of brown rice or the ground; or that of sincerity or concentration. Then little by little I began editing. It was a slow process. I decided early on to preserve the integrity of individual lectures and not cut and paste.

First I went through making minimal changes: removing the "ums" and the "you knows," and making one sentence where Suzuki may have begun a sentence two or three times before settling on a way to say what he wanted to say. From this I edited out the repetitions, which work so well in a lecture, deciding that with the written word readers could always go back and re-read anything they hadn't gotten the first time. A third time through the lectures I tightened up the structure of the talks, aiming to preserve Suzuki's idiosyncratic use of language: "shoulds" and "musts"; many "kind ofs," as in, "this kind of practice" or "this kind of understanding"; a great deal of switching around between "you" and "we"; tense changes; frequent use of "some," usually to indicate an article: "a," "an," or "the."

Although I wanted to preserve Suzuki Roshi's voice as much as possible, I eventually began to edit many of his Japanese-isms and put them into more commonly used English. For instance, many of the should statements became "you" statements or simple imperatives: "You should wake up" might become, "Wake up." Before I got very far in this process, I began working with Sojun Mel Weitsman, another of Suzuki Roshi's disciples, and together we went through the lectures, clarifying the use of "we" or "you," standardizing verb tenses, inserting appropriate articles. Again, although we intended to preserve as much of Suzuki Roshi's language as possible, at the same time we aimed for clarity and readability, hopefully without sacrificing content.

Working together, with both of us agreeing to any changes, gave us the confidence to proceed, and we discovered that we shared a similar sensibility for how to present the material for this book.

Eventually other people read the manuscript: Linda Hess, Carol Williams, Laurie Schley, Norman Fischer, Michael Wenger, Michael Katz. After each reading I would go through the editorial suggestions, then Mel and I would go through them and decide whether or not and how to respond to them. Again, our intention was to preserve Roshi's language while making the minimal number of "corrections" or "clarifications." Sometimes there was nothing we could do to answer, "This isn't clear" or "I don't get this." Sometimes it seemed best simply to let people ponder the Roshi's words.

Now that the process is near completion, I realize that the final results are quite different from the original transcriptions. I hope and trust that we have done justice to the original talks; but while I have no way to make an independent evaluation of our efforts (and Suzuki Roshi suggests more than once that an objective approach may not be especially useful), I do know that I (with Mel's gracious and generous assistance and support) proceeded with care and caution, going slowly, step by step. For those who wish to study the lectures in their most unedited versions, these are available in the library at Zen Center, and we may eventually publish them in that format.

In my efforts to preserve and present Suzuki Roshi's teaching to the public, I felt confident that I was continuing his efforts to present Buddhism to those of us who were his students. However, if there are errors, lapses, or inconsistencies, I accept responsibility. I trust that readers will be forgiving.

Any added comments that are not Suzuki Roshi's words are marked off with brackets.

Some Japanese words used often throughout the manuscript — notably shikantaza, zazen, kinhin, sesshin, and zendo — are not italicized. Brief explanations of these words are in the Introduction. Other foreign words are italicized and explained in the text.

Perhaps my previous experience with *The Tassajara Bread Book* was useful after all. When I set out in 1985 to revise the book, which had originally been published in 1970, I discovered that I had unknowingly written the whole book in Suzuki Roshi English: "Put bread on board and knead with hands." As with a number of students who spent time with him, I had unconsciously learned to speak the way he spoke. I had unknowingly left out most of the articles and pronouns. In fifteen years no one had said anything to me. I decided to put the articles and pronouns back in: "Put the bread on a board and knead it with your hands." In the more than fifteen years since then, no one has said anything to me. What to do? Is one truer? or more direct? Or is it a manner of speaking that I or Suzuki Roshi would correct if we knew better? I cannot say for sure, but I followed my heart and my love for Roshi and his teaching.

Jusan Kainei (Longevity Mountain, Peaceful Sea)
Edward Espe Brown
May, 2001

Further Reading

Brown, Edward Espe. *The Tassajara Bread Book*. Shambhala, revised 1986.

_____. *The Tassajara Recipe Book*. Shambhala, revised 2000.

_____. *Tomato Blessings and Radish Teachings: Recipes and Reflections*. Riverhead Books, 1997.

Chadwick, David. *Crooked Cucumber: The Life and Zen Teaching of Shunryu Suzuki*. Broadway Books, 1999.

_____. *To Shine One Corner of the World: Moments with Shunryu Suzuki*. Broadway Books, 2001.

Suzuki, Shunryu. *Branching Streams Flow in the Darkness: Lectures on the Sandokai*. University of California Press, 1999.

_____. *Zen Mind, Beginner's Mind*. Weatherhill, 1970.

Wind Bell: Teachings from the San Francisco Zen Center, 1968–2001. North Atlantic Books, 2002.

Acknowledgments

I began practicing zazen at Zen Center in 1965, so I am profoundly indebted to hundreds of people with whom I have sat silently over the years. It's not easy being a human being, and the support of others sitting quietly — perhaps we could say, "sorting through their stuff" — seems imperative for the work of "settling the self on the self."

Several people at Zen Center: Mel Weitsman, Norman Fischer, and Michael Wenger, among others, expressed confidence in my editing Suzuki Roshi's lectures. Without their support I never would have started on my own. We have all known each other for thirty years or more. In a variety of contexts and circumstances we have encountered one another's strengths and weaknesses, clarity and dark spots. I embarked on this project because they believed in me.

During the process of selecting and editing lectures I have kept in touch especially with these three people. Mel and I have together gone through every lecture at least once and sometimes three or four times. After our sessions we would enjoy lunch and each other's company. Michael has followed the project all the way through and with surprisingly small gestures and comments has had a profound effect. Norman read through an early version of several lectures and supplied editorial comments with his usual good humor, honesty, and straightforwardness. And his confidence in my abilities has been infectious. Michael Katz, who has been the book agent for both Zen Center and myself, has in his idiosyncratic way nursed the project along. When we visit on the phone it may or may not be about Suzuki Roshi—usually it isn't —but I feel alive, awake, and revitalized.

Linda Hess, Carol Williams, and Laurie Schley read through the manuscript at various stages (a year or more apart) and offered editorial comments. Each had a particular perspective which has been indispensable in refining my own eye and ear for the material. I feel very grateful.

I studied with Reb Anderson for several years and appreciate his wisdom and support. I have also been a student of Jack Kornfield from time to time, and Jack's warm-hearted enthusiasm for my work has been a big encouragement.

Bill Redican's work on the Suzuki Roshi Archive, cataloguing, transcribing, and tracking has been invaluable. His amazing eye and ear for detail and accuracy have considerably improved the manuscript. And of course the archive project is happening largely because of David Chadwick's passion for making Suzuki Roshi's life and teaching available to a wide audience.

Hugh Van Dusen and David Semanki at HarperCollins have been wonderfully supportive.

While not participating in this project directly, Mitsu Suzuki, Suzuki Roshi's widow, will always have a special place in my heart. She has been an inspiration, a teacher, a caretaker. How unfathomable the depth of her devotion and warmheartedness— no green tea has ever tasted better than at her table.

Blessings to everyone,

Edward Brown
Jusan Kainei
May, 2001